HOLLOW
RESISTANCE
OBAMA, TRUMP AND THE
POLITICS OF APPEASEMENT

CounterPunch
PO Box 228
Petrolia, CA 95558
www.counterpunch.org

AK Press
370 Ryan Avenue #100
Chico, CA 95973
www.akpress.org

ISBN: 978-1-939202-35-2
E-ISBN: 978-1-939202-34-5
Library of Congress Control Number: 2018932447

Typography and design by Tiffany Wardle.

Typeset in Minion Pro, designed by
Robert Slimbach for Adobe Systems Inc.
and Founders Grotesk, designed by Kris
Sowersby for Klim Type Foundry.

HOLLOW
RESISTANCE

OBAMA, TRUMP AND THE
POLITICS OF APPEASEMENT

PAUL STREET

TABLE OF CONTENTS

ACKNOWLEDGMENTS

If someone had told me six months ago that I would soon be writing my third book with Barack Obama's name in the title, I would have laughed.

But when a great progressive leader like Ralph Nader speaks, I listen.

I owe the idea for this volume to Nader, for whom I have voted in at least three presidential elections.

The notion that I might be the person to write it belongs to *CounterPunch* editors Joshua Frank and Jeffrey St. Clair.

Understanding the Obama post-presidency is impossible without a firm grasp of the Donald Trump presidency. I am indebted to St. Clair and Frank for granting me access to an excellent, widely consulted venue—the *CounterPunch* website—in which to reflect on the lethal nightmare that became the "Covid45" White House this year.

My earliest writings on and against the Obama phenomenon (dating back sixteen years) were encouraged, inspired, and published by the brilliant radical commentators Bruce Dixon and Glen Ford at *Black Agenda Report* and by *ZNet* and *Z Magazine*'s venerable leaders Mike Albert and Lydia Sargent.

My contributions to radical and real-time Obama historiography (an often thankless field) have long been informed and stimulated by the writings and support of leading Left intellectuals, including John Pilger, Cornel West, Noam Chomsky, Chris Hedges, Adolph Reed, Jr., Charles Derber, and Anthony DiMaggio.

I am deeply indebted to the excellent professional copy-editing and content suggestions of Lucy Schiller. Ms. Schiller made invaluable contributions to the readability of this text on remarkably short notice.

My fellow portside historian and journalist Terry Thomas put forward numerous angles of interpretation and advanced many sources that shaped my narrative and argument. Terry also gave my manuscript an early, highly skilled copy-edit.

Joshua Frank has been the indispensable intermediary and coordinator in bringing this project to completion.

I indebted also to Jay Becker, Lou Downey, and numerous other dedicated activists in the Chicago chapter of Refuse Fascism. Since Trump's election, they have modeled actual and authentic popular resistance in ways that have richly informed my argument and narrative.

Thanks are due also to the many thousands of young people (including some of my "History of Chicago" students at DePaul University) who rose up in a great popular rebellion after the racist lynching of George Floyd in the summer of 2020. I have marched, chanted, occupied intersections, and faced down police and state troopers with young adults and teenagers (and a few oldsters) on numerous occasions in Iowa City and Chicago this summer.

The George Floyd uprising was a needed reminder of what real mass and grassroots resistance looks, feels, sounds, smells, and tastes like (I shared tear gas with a few hundred people less than half my age in Iowa City in early June) and how different such resistance is from the "hollow resistance" advanced by Obama, Joe Biden, and other establishment elites in the corporate Democratic Party.

My greatest debt is to my wife, Janet Razbadouski, who models natural and spiritual intelligence and repeatedly saves me from falling too far down the black hole of American politics.

Paul Street
Chicago, Illinois,
August 4, 2020.

INTRODUCTION
No CounterPunch

During his years in the White House, the sports fanatic Barack Obama adorned the Oval Office with a large framed print of the iconic photograph showing the young boxer Muhammad Ali standing ferociously over the prone body of Sonny Liston after Ali knocked Liston down for the count in a 1965 heavyweight championship match. Obama relished the imagery of a fierce fighter: the charismatic Ali's decimation of Liston, who was emblematic of the ghettoized Black population[1] that had long made Obama uncomfortable.

But when it has come to Donald Trump, Obama's vicious white nationalist successor, where has Obama's counterpunch been? After all, Trump rode to presidential victory after years spent questioning Obama's citizenship, and has since spent much of his administration lashing out at the nation's first Black president. A recent anecdote proves illuminating here. In May of 2020, a paid message appeared in online political publications asking readers to add their name to an online card that read as follows: "THANK PRESIDENT OBAMA: Barack Obama Just Announced That He's Getting Involved to Defeat Trump in 2020!" The thank-you card, featuring a picture of Obama smiling and waving, was sponsored by an organization called "Stop Republicans." I found this message two-thirds of the way into a *POLITICO* essay reporting that Obama's former Vice President and the current presumptive corporate Democratic presidential nominee Joe Biden—whose successful candidacy owed a great deal to Obama—had been compelled to apologize for yet another one of this many foolish campaign gaffes: on this occasion telling the Black radio personality Charlamagne tha God that "If you have a problem figuring out whether you're for me or Trump, then you ain't black."[2]

By "getting involved to defeat Trump in 2020," Stop Republicans was referring to Obama's endorsement of Biden in mid-April, using a boxing analogy to uphold "Joe" as "someone whose own life has taught him how to persevere, how to *bounce back when you have been knocked down*." Obama identified Biden with the call for "a more generous, more democratic America where everybody has a fair shot at opportunity"—standard bourgeois Obama rhetoric.

The "Stop Republicans" thank-you card elicited dark laughter among many of us who had been fighting the Trump-Pence regime in the streets and/or elsewhere in the public sphere since the combination of shady real estate mogul and the right-wing Indiana extremist assumed office in January 2017. Where had the onetime "community organizer" Barack Obama been for the last three-plus years, as the United States plunged ever further into an authoritarian, arch-plutocratic, disease-ridden, and white-nationalist gloom cast by the terrible, tangerine-tinted, twitter-tantruming tyrant Trump? "Obama," Reuters' reporter Steve Holland reflected last May, "has largely kept out of the fray even as Trump has blamed him and his Democratic administration for a variety of problems related to having sufficient supplies to battle the pandemic that has killed more than 75,000 Americans."[3]

That was historical understatement. Obama had been staying largely "out of the fray" not just since the onset of the COVID-19 calamity, but since the beginning of the Trump presidency, even as Trump dismantled one Obama program and policy after another and accused Obama of causing nearly every imaginable evil at home and abroad. The 44th president's general silence, interspersed with only an occasional tepid and highly qualified, often indirect response, has been quite notable in the face of Trump's many shocking neofascistic and eco-cidal transgressions and Trump's related nonstop assault on anything and everything Obama.

This book's first two chapters (titled "Is it the Fascist Apocalypse Yet" and "Where's Obama?," respectively) give numerous examples of the pattern: Obama keeping strangely quiet, private, cautious and largely invisible, offering only occasional, carefully hedged, and usually indirect criticisms of Trump as the nation descended into the nightmare of Trumpian-style fascism. This conservative quiescence, broken slightly during the nation's brutally time-staggered election seasons, has persisted as Trump has continued his longstanding fanatical and compulsive personal and political attack on everything Obama, trying to turn his predecessor into a great Black scapegoat for everything wrong with America. Obama's public criticisms of Trump have been few and far between, mainly issued through leaks, rumors, and indirect avenues. This depressing silence has occurred while Obama has (as we shall see in this book's fourth chapter, titled "Playing and Cashing In") hobnobbed with celebrities, indulged his sports fetish with recurrent phone calls to NBA superstars, played with the rich and famous, and joined the nation's obscenely wealthy economic oligarchy through book contracts and speaking fees.

Obama's fight-back has been far less pronounced than what one might think from reading the headlines of numerous corporate media reports on Obama's occasional and mild retorts to Trump and Trumpism. News reporters and editors have tended to relish every remotely critical comment made by Obama on Trump and his policies, selling these comments as far more direct, deep, and potent than they have been. On closer inspection, many of Obama's purported counterpunches are a bit like the punch with which Muhammad Ali (then Cassius Clay) was alleged to have felled Liston in the first round of their 1965 bout: soft and nearly invisible.

Obama's failure to punch back in a meaningful, forceful, and timely fashion has been all-the-more disturbing given Obama's deep complicity in Trump's ascendancy. This book's third chapter (provocatively titled "Barack Von Obombdenburg") recounts how the corporate-Democratic Obama presidency betrayed (as predicted by myself and other left writers and activists familiar with Obama's earlier history) working people, the poor, and minorities in whose name he had campaigned as the candidate of Hope and Change. It shows how Obama's dismal, corporate—and Wall Street-friendly years in the White House helped demobilize and depress the nation's all-too silenced progressive majority in ways that produced dangerous political openings for an ever more apocalyptic and authoritarian, white-nationalist Republican Party—a party that united behind a lethally ignorant malignant narcissist and at least instinctual fascist (Trump) who was largely under the influence and direction of actual and conscious fascists (Steve Bannon and Stephen Miller) in the summer of 2016. This chapter also shows how Obama bequeathed a number of dangerous authoritarian powers and other deadly tools and tendencies to the lethal autocrat.

One of the supreme ironies of Obama's post-presidential popularity (astronomical among Democrats) is that it is a product of the disastrous Trump administration, which Obama himself played a key role in producing, and which has both burnished and even whitewashed Obama's legacy. Before he did so much to accommodate the horrific Trump White House, Obama helped create it. What liberals who wear with t-shirts showing Obama's smiling face asking "Miss Me Yet?" will not or cannot admit is that the Trumpenstein is Obama's creation, and to no small extent.

Obama's meekness has been yet more distressing given his high approval ratings and his status as what *The Atlantic*'s Vann R. Newkirk II aptly called in the summer of 2018 "a sort of make-believe president in exile for the political opposition in America."[4] With his legacy buffed by the awfulness of a presidency he helped birth, Obama now polls as "more popular than Jesus" among

Democrats. As the leading target of Trump's relentless Orwellian distortion and as a political figure held in high esteem by most Americans, Obama would have been well positioned to speak up forcefully against Trump and Trumpism these last three plus terrible years.

Adding insult to injury, Obama has held at least one arm behind his back, barely and only occasionally stepping into the ring while quietly climbing into the nation's grotesquely opulent economic aristocracy. This book's fourth chapter, titled "Playing, Cashing In," dives into the sordid story of the material and lifestyle rewards that Obama received from his friends in the American ruling class, even as Trump drove the nation into unprecedented nightmarish depths.

Adding even more insult and injury to the growing pile, Obama has helped clear the way for a second Trump term or perhaps a future presidency even more dangerously and consciously white-nationalist than Trump's (Tom Cotton 2025?) by working behind the scenes (again) to defeat the progressive wing of his own party and nominate the gaffe-prone, right-wing corporate Democrat and arch-imperialist Joe Biden—an uninspiring and lackluster, not to mention conservative, presidential candidate if ever there's been one. This is the subject of Chapter 5, titled "Joe Biden? Thanks, Obama".

All of this is richly consistent with Obama's prior and deeply conservative history, as I show in Chapter 6, titled "Obama Being Obama: A Hollow Man Filled with Ruling Class Ideas". Like President Obama, post-White House Obama has been precisely the center-right ruling-class operative that I and other Left activists and intellectuals have tried to warn liberals and progressives about since the very beginning of his political career. Obama's noxious role during the Trump years have been richly consistent not only with his presidency but with his deeply conservative nature, which traces well back before his time in the White House.

The book's conclusion addresses Lenin's famous question: "what is to be done?" It tackles the lethal reactionary consequences of the "Lesser Evil Voting" syndrome that plagues U.S. liberals, progressive and leftists every four years—and of the entire deeply flawed U.S. party and elections system. It reflects also on what a meaningful and authentic popular resistance and genuinely oppositional politics might look like beneath and beyond the quadrennial big money major media candidate-centered, corporate-managed, mass-marketed electoral extravaganzas that are sold to Americans as "that's politics"—the only politics that matters. These reflections hold, the present writer maintains, regardless of the election's outcome (assuming the contest is held) this November. They remain no less relevant if Biden succeeds—an outcome not without its own dangerous consequences for the future of America and the world—than if Trump captures a second term.

As a young adult, Obama understood some of what this book argues. But, like numerous aspiring bourgeois elites and rulers before and since, the nation's future and first Black president abandoned the radical and democratic wisdom of youth in pursuit of more "realistic," "practical," and "pragmatic" aims—aims that disingenuously claim the label "progressive" while steering clear of any substantive challenge to the nation's unelected and interrelated dictatorships of money, empire, white supremacy, patriarchy, and ecological plunder. How sad, both for the American people and even, if less consequentially, for Obama himself.

The research for this book was completed on August 1, 2020, at a time when it had become for the first time commonplace in mainstream liberal media to hear Trump and his presidency mentioned as potentially or already "fascist" and "fascistic." The last Obama statement that I was able to cover and reflect upon in this volume was the former president's widely heralded oration at the nationally televised state funeral of Congressman John Lewis on July 30, 2020. Readers interested in my reflections on subsequent developments germane to the subject matter(s) of this book should consult my author page at *CounterPunch* (https://www.counterpunch.org/author/paul-street/) and my personal website (www.paulstreet.org).

ENDNOTES

1. David Remnick, *King of the World: Muhammad Ali and the Rise of an American Hero…*

2. Quint Forgey and Myah Ward, "Biden Apologizes for his Controversial 'You Ain't Black Comment,'" *POLITICO*, May 22, 2020, https://www.politico.com/news/2020/05/22/joe-biden-breakfast-club-interview-274490?fbclid=IwAR3x-pYkoXuFMu2k9bH-xhRMW1vILposfE9zgBS0CJqPSAM2mdkwjKAYLeFk

3. Steve Holland, "In Leaked Call, Obama Describes Trump Handling of Virus as Chaotic," *Reuters*, May 9, 2020, https://www.reuters.com/article/us-usa-trump-obama/in-leaked-call-obama-describes-trump-handling-of-virus-as-chaotic-idUSKBN22L0ST

4. Vann R. Newkirk, II, "Barack Obama Still Doesn't Understand Trump," *The Atlantic*, July 20, 2018.

CHAPTER ONE
Is it the Fascist Apocalypse Yet?
This Happened Here

> The point, though, is, is that we all go forward, with a presumption of good faith in our fellow citizens—because that presumption of good faith is essential to a vibrant and functioning democracy.
> —President Barack Obama, speaking in the Rose Garden the day after Trump was elected

> Tim, remember, his is no time to be a purist. You've got to keep *a fascist* out of the White House.
> —President Barack Obama, speaking to the Democratic Party's vice-presidential candidate Tim Kaine in October 2016.

> I don't believe in the apocalyptic—until the apocalypse comes. I think nothing is the end of the world until the end of the world.
> —President Barack Obama, speaking to *New Yorker* editor David Remnick days after Trump was elected.

> Hitler was not dedicated with fervor to destroying the prospects of organized human life on Earth in the not-distant future (along with millions of other species). Trump is.
> —Noam Chomsky, February 2020

"NO APOCALYPSE" BECAUSE "WE ARE ALL ON THE SAME TEAM"

Barack Obama's accommodation of Donald Trump's noxious presidency started even before Trump took to power. Obama, to use historian Margaret George's phrase,[1] was a "hollow man," a master of vapid, patriotic, and bipartisan platitudes, delivered in a distinctively clipped and sanctimonious tone. His speech the day after Donald Trump's shocking victory proved no exception.

While the election results reverberated through a disbelieving and bewildered media, Obama went out to the White House Rose Garden to, in the trademark language of his public relations department, "address the nation on the election results and the next steps we can take to come together as a country and ensure a peaceful transition of power."

Obama had just finished telling young White House staffers he had called to the Oval Office that "this is not the apocalypse." When *The New Yorker's* editor David Remnick asked Obama about that consoling remark two days later, Obama said "I don't believe in the apocalyptic—until the apocalypse comes. I think nothing is the end of the world until the end of the world."[2]

Obama's oration that day was a *tour de force* of accommodation, appeasement, and denial. He called for a "peaceful transition" to power for the next president, whom he knew to be a fascist, a malignant racist who had spent years claiming Obama was born outside the U.S., and who launched his campaign with a racist assault on Mexicans. Despite Trump's history of vicious attacks, Obama spoke in muted terms of conservatism, unity, and normalization:

> Now, everybody is sad when their side loses an election. But the day after, we have to remember that *we're actually all on one team. This is an intramural scrimmage. We're not Democrats first. We're not Republicans first. We are Americans first. We're patriots first. We all want what's best for this country. That's what I heard in Mr. Trump's remarks last night. That's what I heard when I spoke to him directly.* And I was heartened by that. That's what the country needs—a sense of unity; a sense of inclusion; a respect for our institutions, our way of life, rule of law; and a respect for each other. I hope that he maintains that spirit throughout this transition, and I certainly hope that's how his presidency has a chance to begin.

> …A lot of our fellow Americans are exultant today. A lot of Americans are less so. But that's the nature of campaigns. *That's the nature of democracy.* It is hard, and sometimes

contentious and noisy, and it's not always inspiring…
Sometimes *you lose an argument.* Sometimes you lose an
election. The path that this country has taken has never
been a straight line. We zig and zag, and sometimes we
move in ways that some people think is forward and others
think is moving back. And that's okay. I've lost elections
before.

That's the way politics works sometimes. *We try really hard
to persuade people that we're right. And then people vote.* And
then if we lose, we learn from our mistakes, we do some
reflection, we lick our wounds, we brush ourselves off, we
get back in the arena. We go at it. We try even harder the
next time.

The point, though, is, is *that we all go forward, with a presumption of good faith in our fellow citizens—because that presumption of good faith is essential to a vibrant and functioning
democracy.* That's how this country has moved forward for
240 years. It's how we've pushed boundaries and promoted
freedom around the world. That's how we've expanded the
rights of our founding to reach all of our citizens. It's how
we have come this far.

And that's why I'm confident that *this incredible journey
that we're on as Americans will go on. And I am looking
forward to doing everything that I can to make sure that the
next President is successful in that. I have said before, I think
of this job as being a relay runner—you take the baton, you
run your best race, and hopefully, by the time you hand it off
you're a little further ahead, you've made a little progress.* And
I can say that we've done that, and I want to make sure that
handoff is well-executed, because ultimately we're all on the
same team. [Author's emphasis added.]

This speech, delivered after Trump's victory, was Obama's standard bromide-laden style. It hammered away at the supposed
"democratic" greatness of America and the shared visions and
values of all Americans regardless of race, color, creed, gender,
nationality, class, and party. These, too, were the same old tired
nostrums Obama and many of his fans had been confusing with
Lincolnesque eloquence ever since he arrived on the national

political stage in the summer of 2004. Reflecting on Hillary Clinton's equally accommodating concession speech, the brilliant expatriate Masha Gessen's words could be easily applied to Obama's Rose Garden oration:

> It was as though Donald Trump had not, in the course of his campaign, promised to deport US citizens, promised to create a system of surveillance targeted specifically at Muslim Americans, promised to build a wall on the border with Mexico, advocated war crimes, endorsed torture, and repeatedly threatened to jail Hillary Clinton herself. It was as though those statements and many more could be written off as so much campaign hyperbole and now that the campaign was over, Trump would be eager to become a regular, rule-abiding politician of the pre-Trump era.

Yet there was someone else who knew very well that Barack Obama and Hillary Clinton's concessionary statements were historically off-base: *Barack Obama*. While Obama was and is many unpleasant things, stupid and uninformed are not among them. He certainly had no genuine personal confidence in Trump's respect for democracy, the rule of law, his opponents, common decency, or "our institutions." Indeed, Obama knew quite a bit. He knew very well that Trump did not want "what's best for this country." He knew that the President Elect and his Trumpenvolk followers deserved no "presumption of good faith." Obama certainly knew very well that Trump and his base[3] were driven by racist, sexist, authoritarian, nativist, militarist and eco-exterminist beliefs and impulses, and not by any commitment to "expand[ing] the rights of our founding" and "promot[ing] freedom" at home or abroad—quite the opposite. Obama was surely aware that Trump had nothing to do with "mov[ing] this country forward." He knew that Trump was an enemy of a "vibrant and functioning democracy" and a symptom of the absence of any such "democracy" in corporate-ruled America, a country that had yet to constitutionally introduce the popular election of its top official (the highly unpopular Trump had lost the technically irrelevant popular tally by 3 million votes to the also widely despised Hillary Clinton, making him the fifth U.S. president selected by the openly undemocratic Electoral College but not by the plurality of voting citizens). Obama knew that Trump's victory was not achieved by a healthy democratic debate in which reasoned arguments were presented and the democratic voice of the people was heard. And he knew that Trump had no intention of "uniting the country" across party, racial, ethnic, geographic, ideological, and economic lines. Quite the opposite!

A FASCIST IN THE WHITE HOUSE

As we know from *Hillary,* a Hillary Clinton documentary released last January, then-president Obama called Donald Trump a "fascist" in an October 2016 conversation with Hillary Clinton's then-running mate, Senator Tim Kaine. "Tim, remember," Obama said by phone, "this is no time to be a purist. You've got to keep *a fascist* out of the White House."[4]

Speaking to *New Yorker* editor David Remnick on a campaign trip to North Carolina four days before the election, Obama said "We've seen this coming. Donald Trump is not an outlier; he is a culmination, a logical conclusion of the rhetoric and tactics of the Republican Party for the past ten, fifteen, twenty years… we've seen it for eight years, even with reasonable people like John Boehner, who, when push came to shove, wouldn't push back against these currents."

Early in Obama's first term, as hateful right-wing white-nationalist opposition developed under the name of the Republican Tea Party, law professor Phyllis Bernard aptly described one of the aforementioned currents as "eliminationism," the belief that one's political opponents are "a cancer on the body politic that must be excised—either by separation from the public at large, through censorship or by outright extermination—in order to protect the purity of the nation."

Obama was no fool. He had read enough history and political science, and had also personally experienced enough vicious racist, Birtherist, nativist targeting by Trump, to know very well that the next president and most of his allies and backers had no real "good faith" respect for the rule of law, for social "inclusion," for solidarity across racial and ethnic lines, or for the common good at home and abroad. Moreover, Obama was too astute and educated not to have known what *The New Yorker*'s Adam Gopnik powerfully highlighted in May of 2016:

> There is a simple formula for descriptions of Donald Trump: add together a qualification, a hyphen, and the word "fascist" …his personality and his program belong exclusively to the same dark strain of modern politics: an incoherent program of *national revenge led by a strongman; a contempt for parliamentary government and procedures; an insistence that the existing, democratically elected government…is in league with evil outsiders and has been secretly trying to undermine the nation; a hysterical militarism designed to no particular end other than the sheer spectacle of strength; an equally hysterical sense of beleaguerment and victimization; and a supposed suspicion of big capitalism entirely reconciled to the worship of wealth and 'success.'… The idea that it can be bounded in by honest conservatives in a Cabinet or restrained by normal constitutional limits is, to put it mildly, unsupported by history.* [Emphasis added][5]

These were prophetic words. Something like an "apocalypse" emerged from Trump's ascendancy into the White House. Consistent with his toxic 2015–16 presidential campaign and with his earlier career in public life, Trump's presidency has from the beginning displayed numerous overlapping characteristics of historical fascism, broadly understood: constant propaganda to mask objectionable goals with widely accepted ideals; fairy-tale notions of a glorious national past of patriarchal racial purity betrayed by elites; "us and them" scapegoating of demonized Others and foreigners; relentless attacks on intellectuals, expertise, and reasoned public discourse; constant assault on the public's capacity to perceive reality and agree on truth; the promotion and glorification of traditional social and political hierarchy; unceasing bombardments on the rule of law; rejection of constitutional and parliamentary checks and balances; a Social Darwinian fixation on false binaries like triumph vs. defeat, thriving vs. failing, strength vs. weakness, and "greatness" vs. inferiority; demonization of the free press; promotion of a cult of personality; hyper-militarism; glorification of violence; the embrace of violence against political enemies and critics; performative pomp; theatrical gatherings; the dehumanization of racial, ethnic, religious, cultural Others and political enemies; emotionally potent and extreme statements (the "greatest ever," the "worst ever," "amazing," "horrible" and so on); recurrent menacing rallies; the assertion of instinct and will over reason and thought; the purging of the disloyal; a false populist posture that obscures service to and alliance with capitalist elites and capitalism; fierce anti-socialism; the gleeful degradation of women and ongoing assault on women's rights; attacks on gay rights and transgendered people; the demonization and false conflation of liberals and "the Left;" and a predilection for bizarre, offensive conspiracy theories such as the notion that the Jewish Elders of Zion and George Soros are secretly controlling world events.[6]

As if another list was needed that detailed the overlap between fascism and the strategies of the Trump administration, a book published by a leading civil rights lawyer last year found twenty common themes, tactics, and policies that Trump was "copying from the early Hitler government" in 1930s Germany: holding power without winning majority support; finding and using direct lines of communication with their base; blaming others and dividing along racial lines; relentlessly demonizing opponents; constantly attacking objective truth; relentlessly attacking mainstream media; assaulting science; cultivating a fawning alternative media to spread lies; regular orchestrated mass hate-rallies; extreme nationalism; closing borders; embracing

mass detention and deportation; using borders to protect selected industries; embedding authoritarian rule by rewarding capitalist elites; rejecting international norms; attacking domestic
democratic processes; attacking courts and the rule of law; glo-
rifying the military and demanding loyalty oaths; proclaiming
unchecked power; relegating women to subordinate roles.

Pundits have routinely noticed Trump's special love for
despots and dictators of various ideological stripes (ranging
from Vladimir Putin and the blood-soaked Filipino strongman Rodrigo Duterte to the murderous Saudi Crown Prince
Mohammad bin-Salman, the North Korean dictator Kim Jong-
Un, the Brazilian eco-Nazi Jair Bolsonaro, and Turkish despot
Recep Erdogan) around the world. The reason is obvious. "The
president," one top national security aide told the senior Trump
administration official "Anonymous," "sees in these guys what he
wishes he had: total power, no term limits, enforced popularity,
and the ability to silence critics for good."

It was chilling to read this quote in the wake of the Republican
Senate's blatantly authoritarian and frankly absurd decision to
exonerate Trump even prior to his 2019 impeachment trial, drop-
ping even the threat of removal from the proceedings. Caught
red-handed trying to trade arms to Ukraine in return for political
dirt on his presidential rival Joe Biden, Trump escaped removal
or even censure for UkraineGate, a monumentally criminal abuse
of presidential power, because his white-nationalist party made
a mockery of the U.S. Constitution by refusing to hear witnesses
and consider new evidence in a Senate "trial" that could only
be described as a farce. Trump's successful argument for "exon-
eration" included the chilling claim by Trump's risible celebrity
attorney Alan Dershowitz that the president could do anything
he wanted if he believed it would help his re-election.

LIVE AND LET DIE

On the heels of the hyper-partisan impeachment travesty came Trump's miserable and botched response to the COVID-19 crisis. With deadly consequences for hundreds of thousands of vulnerable Americans, Trump failed to take the pandemic seriously. In March and April of 2020, the U.S. body count rapidly rose to the highest in the world—a darkly ironic twist on Trump's neofascist slogan "America First." As the cases mounted, Trump refused to order an appropriate testing regime or to mandate the adequate production and provision of medical and protective equipment. Leaving much of the nation's response to state governors, Trump initially called the novel coronavirus a hoax, claiming that it would magically "disappear" soon and recommending quack cures. He fired a top pandemic response expert and official, Dr. Rick Bright, for raising alarms about the shortage of masks and other protective gear. He applauded right-wing militia activists who brought assault weapons to state capitols to protest common-sense shutdowns, masking regulations, and social distancing measures meant to save lives.

Trump's lethal response combined his usual mix of toxic ingredients: nationalist xenophobia (referring to COVID-19 as "the China Virus," later renamed by him as "the Kung Flu"), nativism (including a suspension of legal immigration to the U.S., issued on Adolph Hitler's birthday), conspiracy, and a cold indifference to the plight of American workers and minorities as well as the elderly.

The president's fascistic callousness was on sickening display when he visited a prematurely re-opened Arizona mask factory. Trump pretentiously refused to wear a mask while talking to company officials, all of whom were masked. The macabre scene was presented to the public with Guns and Roses' version of the darkly appropriate tune "Live and Let Die" blaring in the background.

Pandemic-related death hung over workers in other plants as well. In the meatpacking industry, more than 25,000 disproportionately Latinx workers were infected and 91 died from COVID-19 by mid-June of 2020. These terrible numbers increased fivefold after Trump issued an April 28 executive order reopening slaughterhouses and meat processing plants after the spread of the virus forced the closure of dozens of plants.

Moreover, early reports showed that COVID-19 was wreaking the worst havoc on Black Americans. But anyone who thought Trump would be moved to take appropriate protective action was mistaken. If anything, Trump and his chief political adviser, the neofascist white-nationalist Stephen Miller, were likely encouraged to accelerate the "opening up" and "liberation" of the country by the news that the virus was particularly decimating people of color.

As the United States set a grim new record with 50,000 new cases on July 1st, 2020, a reflection of his mind-boggling inaction and incompetence, Trump continued with one of his recurrent themes: that the coronavirus would miraculously vanish at some point. "We're heading back in a very strong fashion," he told FOX Business News on July 1, "and I think we're going to be very good with the coronavirus. I think at some point that's going to sort of just disappear, I hope."[7]

Within days, Trump falsely and irresponsibly claimed that 99 percent of coronavirus cases were "totally harmless" and that the rising number of U.S. COVID-19 cases were a result simply of increased testing. Meanwhile, the Trump administration absurdly insisted that the U.S. was leading the world in responding effectively to the coronavirus—a complete Orwellian inversion of reality as America's case count skyrocketed to record levels in Texas, Arizona, and Florida, and took off across much of the nation's southern and Western sunbelt. Vice President Pence told frontline healthcare workers to re-use PPE—an astonishing statement four months after the coronavirus broke out in the U.S.

Then came the educational offensive. In early July, Trump threatened to ban international students from colleges and universities that failed to fully resume in-person classes in the fall of 2020. He also pressed public schools physically reopen, threatening to withhold federal funding from those districts that deemed the pandemic too dangerous for that. In mid-July, Trump's press secretary said that "The science should not stand in the way of this," adding that it was "perfectly safe" to fully reopen all classrooms.[8]

This was around the same time that the Trump administration launched a purge-style propaganda assault on the nation's leading official infectious disease expert Dr. Anthony Fauci. Irked by Fauci's failure to go along with the White House's Orwellian claims to be leading the world in responding positively to the COVID-19 crisis, the administration publicly released what amounted to opposition research on Fauci's real and alleged mistakes in responding to the novel coronavirus. The attack had nothing to do with public health. It was an effort to downgrade Fauci's high public approval, which was seen as a threat to Trump's re-election.

In mid-July, Americans learned that hospital data on coronavirus patients was being rerouted to the Trump administration instead of first being sent to the U.S. Centers for Disease Control and Prevention (the CDC). This profoundly dangerous and authoritarian move made critical medical data less transparent to the public as Trump continued to mass-murderously downplay the accelerating spread of the pandemic.

Around the same time, the Trump White House introduced sweeping loyalty tests for the nation's public health officials, asking them if they were sufficiently devoted to the president.[9]

And so, as the world looked aghast at the United States' shocking failure to rise to the deadly occasion, it seemed to many that "the apocalypse" Obama told his staff wasn't coming with Trump had, in fact, arrived.

THE WORD IS DOMINATE

In the midst of the COVID-19 crisis, the nation and world beheld Trump's despicably racist, authoritarian, and fascist reaction to the remarkable surge of civil rights and social justice protests that arose after George Floyd, a 42-year old Black man, was murdered by white police officers in Minneapolis in late May of 2020. Caught on cell phone video, the horrific lynching of Floyd sparked a mass, largely youthful uprising, which police met with tear gas and other violent anti-protest tactics in more than one hundred U.S. cities and towns.

Trump's response to the nationwide anti-racist rebellions was nothing less than fascist. "'When the looting starts,' Trump Tweeted, placing quote marks around the phrase after rioting broke out within and beyond Minneapolis, 'the shooting starts.'" Those words were first spoken by Walter Headley, the racist white chief of Miami's police, in 1967.

"Rather than focus on protesters' grievances—such as systemic racism and police brutality—Trump," NBC News reported, "turned his focus to squelching the civil unrest that has accompanied the national demonstrations and has taken a hardline stance to restoring order." Many reporters seemed surprised and even shocked by the president's "hardline" response. But they should have expected it. Why would Trump, a cold-blooded "law and order" racist who had long been telling cops to "take the gloves off" and harshly punish people of color, have listened with empathy to protesters' cries against structural racism and police violence? And "taking a hardline stance to restoring order" was putting it mildly. On Monday, June 1, Trump berated the nation's governors in a conference call, calling them "weak" in the face of the rebellions. "If you don't dominate [the protests]," Trump said, "you're wasting your time." Further:

> In Washington, they had large groups, very large groups. ...
> But we're going to have it under much more control. We're
> pouring in—we're going to pull in thousands of people...

> We're going to clamp down very, very strong. The word is dominate. If you don't dominate your city and your state, they're gonna walk away with you. And we're doing it in Washington, in DC, we're going to do something that people haven't seen before. … we're going to have total domination.

> "Law enforcement response is not going to work," Trump's authoritarian Attorney General William Barr told the governors, "unless we dominate the streets."

"Total domination" was the language of the supreme dictator who Trump clearly dreamed of becoming. Trump told the governors that "you have to use the military" and "we have a wonderful military." He described the 2011 Occupy Wall Street movement as a "disgrace" that was rightly ended by governors and mayors being "tough." He told the governors that protesters should serve ten-year prison sentences. Meanwhile, Trump's top military official, U.S. Defense Secretary Mark Esper, said this to a new domestic riot-control "central command center" headed Joint Chiefs Chair Gen. Mark Milley, Esper, and Attorney General William Barr: "The sooner that you mass and dominate the battlespace the sooner this dissipates and we can get back to the right normal."

An interesting term, "the right normal"—that's when the nation's citizens stay home and cower while police, prison guards, border guards, and other public officials, including the president, murder and maim poor people, workers, and people of color with impunity, both directly and indirectly.

After his "total domination" harangue, Trump ordered combat-ready military personnel to Washington D.C. from Fort Bragg in North Carolina. He threatened protesters outside the White House with "vicious dogs" and "ominous weapons." After police and National Guard military police brutally cleared Lafayette Square with chemical weapons and batons to let the wannabe strongman come out of a protective bunker in which Secret Service had placed him on the evening of June 1, Trump gave a nod to the Christian fascists in his base. The deadly clown walked across Pennsylvania Avenue to pose while awkwardly holding up a Holy Bible before cameras at historic St. John's Parish.[10] "We have the greatest country in the world, we're going to keep it nice and safe," Trump proclaimed. Trump never set foot in the church, eschewing an opportunity to pray for peace or for George Floyd. Or for the wisdom to lead the nation in its moment of crisis. Before marching to the church, Trump said this in the White House Rose Garden: "Mayors and governors must establish an overwhelming law enforcement presence until the violence has been quelled. If a city or state refuses to take the actions that are necessary to defend the life and property of their residents, then I will deploy the United States military and quickly solve the problem for them."

Earlier in the day, a senior Pentagon official told the *Washington Post*, Trump stated, "We need to get control of the streets. We need ten thousand troops up here [in Washington]. I want it right now." Trump's far-right evangelical Vice President Mike Pence had argued for invoking the 1807 Insurrection Act.[11]

"Our country always wins," Trump said. "That is why I am taking immediate Presidential action to stop the violence and restore security and safety in America We are putting everybody on warning. . .One law and order and that is what it is. One law—we have one beautiful law."

The demented oligarch went on to falsely accuse the very predominantly peaceful protesters of "the spilling of innocent blood"—an Orwellian inversion of reality if ever there was one. He called protesters' actions "crime[s] against God." Smearing the entire movement as the handiwork of "professional anarchists, violent mobs, arsonists, looters, Antifa, and others," Trump threatened to commit a war crime by turning the US military on and against the public's rights of free speech and assembly. Along the way, he tried to encourage his "MAGA" base of white supporters to come out into the streets to physically confront the protesters for civil and human rights outside the White House.

It was hard for any careful observer not to notice the stark and revealing dichotomy between the president's attitude towards the George Floyd protesters and the president's stance on those right-wing protestors of the stay-at-home and social distancing orders issued by state governors to protect citizens from the pandemic. The heavily racialized hypocrisy could not have been more obvious. When white nationalists armed with assault weapons and body armor occupied the Michigan State Capitol and shutdown the state legislature to demand the "liberation" of their state from coronavirus restrictions in late April of 2020, Trump cheered them on. He repeatedly cited the First (free speech) and Second (gun ownership) Amendments of the U.S. Constitution to support right-wing protests, many of them involving demonstrators toting weapons, against local and state-level coronavirus rules in March and April.

Masha Gessen captured the essence of Trump's response to the Movement for Black Lives rebellion in a commentary titled "Trump's Fascist Performance":

> Donald Trump thinks power looks like masked men in combat uniforms lined up in front of the marble columns of the Lincoln Memorial. He thinks it looks like Black Hawk helicopters hovering so low over protesters that they chop off the tops of trees. He thinks it looks like troops using tear gas to clear a plaza for a photo op. He thinks it looks like him hoisting a Bible in his raised right hand…To Trump, power sounds like the word "dominate," repeated over and over on a leaked call with governors. It sounds like the silence of the men in uniform when they are asked who they are… power grab is always a performance of sorts…In his intuition, power is autocratic; it affirms the superiority of one nation and one race; it asserts total domination; and it mercilessly suppresses all opposition. Whether or not he is capable of grasping the concept, Trump is performing fascism.[12]

"WHITE POWER" AND RACE FEAR

The racist and neofascistic madness of wannabe King Donald peaked in late June and early July as numerous Trump administration officials flatly denied that systemic racism was a problem in the systemically racist United States. During an unhinged two-hour June 20th speech delivered in Tulsa, Oklahoma, in an enclosed event that produced five hundred new coronavirus cases, Trump called the coronavirus "the Kung Flu" and went full-bore with wild QAnon conspiracy theories claiming (among other false and bizarre things) that Joe Biden was under the control of unnamed radical powers and that Biden and the Democrats favored the "after-birth execution" of babies. Trump threatened and promoted violence against liberals and the left and raised the timeworn specter of nonwhite "hombres" raping unprotected white women.

At the end of June, after the anti-racist protests had subsided, Trump posted a tweet of a white senior citizen yelling "White Power" from a golf cart at a Florida retirement community called The Villages. Trump wrote "Thank You to the great people of The Villages," adding a shot at the "Radical Left Do Nothing Democrats."

Also receiving Twitter approval from Trump was a video showing two wealthy white St. Louis personal injury lawyers standing outside their mansion to threaten Black protesters with an assault weapon and a pistol.

Then Trump outdid himself by referring to "Black Lives Matter" as a "symbol of hate." Only Donald Trump could call a statement of affirmation of the lives of Black people a symbol and statement of "hate." Meanwhile, he continued to defend the many statues of Confederate leaders standing across the U.S. South. The monuments, under unprecedented attack in the wake of the Movement for Black Lives rebellions, celebrate the South's treasonous secession from the United States in defense of Black chattel slavery. "You don't want to take away our heritage and history, and the beauty," Trump said, indifferent to the sentiments of Black Americans who were reasonably fed up with seeing public symbols celebrating those who fought to preserve a racist slave system. When asked what he had to say to such Black Americans, Trump said this: "My message is that we have a great country: We have the greatest country on Earth. We have a heritage."

As public monuments honoring the racist and secessionist slaveowners' Confederacy came under attack across the country in the wake of the George Floyd rebellion, Trump repeatedly defended these toxic racist symbols as valuable parts of America's shared historical legacy. He even vetoed the 2020 Pentagon funding bill because it included name changes for military bases previously named after Confederate War heroes."

At the end of July, as this manuscript neared its completion date, Trump took racist "dog-whistling" to a new decibel level by telling a white Texas audience that "the radical Left" wanted to "abolish the suburbs" and "incite riots." Trump boasted to a cheering racist crowd that he had just "ended the rule on suburbs. You know, the suburbs, people fight all their lives to get into the suburbs and have a beautiful home. There will be no more low-income housing forced into the suburbs. ...I just rescinded the rule. It's been going on for years....It's been HELL for suburbia. We rescinded the rule three days ago, so enjoy your life, ladies and gentlemen, enjoy your life."

The policy change referenced in this wild rant? Trump rescinded the Affirmatively Furthering Fair Housing (AFFH) rule, established by the Obama administration in 2015. The rule required any locality that receives block-grant funds from HUD to produce an assessment showing how it would guarantee equal access to housing without racial and other forms of discrimination.

TIME TO SAY THE F-WORD

On the night of July 3, 2020, Trump held a white-nationalist rally that transparently mimicked Nazi Third Reich aesthetics at a Fourth of July celebration event at Mount Rushmore in South Dakota. There were no masks or social distancing required at Trump's speech, in which he "claimed," as CNN reported, "that a left-wing fascist mob was trying to 'end America' by erasing the nation's history and indoctrinating its children."

At a July 4th speech in Washington, D.C. ,Trump said "We are now in the process of defeating the radical left, the Marxists, the anarchists, the agitators, the looters, and people who, in many instances, have absolutely no clue what they are doing." The event highlighted the pageantry and power of the US military while snubbing public health anti-pandemic recommendations.

In early July, Trump threatened the tax-exempt status of American colleges and universities, bizarrely claiming that "Too many universities and school systems are about Radical Left Indoctrination."

It was all very consistent with an under-reported neofascistic Executive Order that Trump signed on June 26, 2020. The president's "Executive Order on Protecting American Monuments, Memorials and Statues and Combating Recent Criminal Violence" sought to justify the repression of civil rights and social protesters by falsely claiming that "innocent citizens" were under attack from "arsonists and left-wing extremists" who "have led riots in the streets, burned police vehicles, killed and assaulted government officers as well as business owners defending their property..." Trump's Order claimed that the George Floyd uprising "paints the United States of America as fundamentally unjust," "shamelessly attack[s] the legitimacy of our institutions," and challenges "the fundamental truth that America is good, her people are virtuous, and that justice prevails in this country to a far greater extent than anywhere else in the world." In an especially ominous passage, Trump targeted "Marxism" in particular, saying that: "Many of the rioters, arsonists, and left-wing extremists who have carried out and supported these acts have explicitly identified themselves with ideologies—such as Marxism—that call for the destruction of the United States' system of government."

As scholars have long observed, fascism relies significantly on the claim that the virtuous Nation is besieged by a powerful radical Left that must be crushed.

Following his wildly distorted and classically fascistic claims that the inherently virtuous national Fatherland was under assault from Left radicals, Trump ordered the following extreme federal penalties for "any person or any entity" [i.e., group or organization] "that destroys, damages, vandalizes, or desecrates a monument, memorial, or statue within the United States or otherwise vandalizes government property": ten years in jail and a $250,000 fine for each count.

Trump didn't stop there, however. His order made the same threat against "any person or entity" that "participates in efforts to incite violence or other illegal activity in connection with the riots and acts of vandalism" and anyone who "assist[s] the agitator" or "aid[s] and abet[s]" others accused of federal crimes is subject to the same penalty. The terms "aid," "abet," and "assist" are very broad, including actions like giving someone a ride or a bottle of water. In essence, the order criminalized the Black Lives Matter protest wave.

Trump's order authorized the deployment of federal paramilitary forces in local areas without requests from local officials. The personnel offered included the U.S. military, Customs and Border Protection, ICE, FBI, and the Secret Service. Days later, the head of the Department of Homeland Security (DHS) announced "the deployment and pre-positioning of Rapid Deployment Teams across the country to respond to potential threats to facilities and property." These teams were sent to a number of cities, including Portland and Seattle, while others were positioned to be within reach anywhere in the U.S. within six hours. Infamously brutal and racist Border Patrol and ICE agents played major roles in these paramilitary teams sent out to protect the Fatherland's monuments and property from "Marxist" and left "extremists."

In early July, Trump and his Attorney General Barr sent more than a hundred paramilitary agents from the Department of Homeland Security to crack down on anti-racist social justice protesters in Portland, where activists had undertaken nightly Black Lives Matter demonstrations since the murder of George Floyd. Code-named "Operation Diligent Valor," the deployment chillingly resembled US military operations abroad. The federal gendarmes, many suspected to be mercenaries on contract from Erik Prince (a close Trump ally and the fascist head of the onetime notorious global mercenary firm Blackwater), swept up protesters into unmarked cars and vans, teargassed crowds, and beat reporters. In mid-July, a federal paramilitary nearly killed a young Portland protester by shooting him in the head with a lethal "impact munition" while the victim had his hands raised. Also shot in the head and sent to an emergency room was Maureen Healy, chair of the History department at Lewis & Clark College and a specialist in the rise of German fascism. While recovering from her injuries, professor Healy wrote the following:

> Since June, I have been attending peaceful protests in Portland neighborhoods in support of Black Lives Matter. I have gone with family and friends.
>
> I am a 52-year-old mother. I am a history professor. I went downtown yesterday to express my opinion as a citizen of the United States, and as a resident of Portland. Of Oregon. This is my home. I was protesting peacefully. So why did federal troops shoot me in the head Monday night?
>
> I was in a large crowd of ordinary folks. Adults, teens, students. Moms and dads. It looked to me like a cross-section of the City. Black Lives Matter voices led the crowd on a peaceful march from the Justice Center past the murals at the Apple store. The marchers were singing songs. We were chanting. We were saying names of Black people that have

been killed by police. We observed a moment of silence in front of the George Floyd mural.

I wanted to, and will continue to, exercise my First Amendment right to speak. Federal troops have been sent to my city to extinguish these peaceful protests. I was not damaging federal property. I was in a crowd with at least a thousand other ordinary people. I was standing in a public space.

In addition to being a Portland resident, I am also a historian. My field is Modern European History, with specialization in the history of Germany and Eastern Europe. I teach my students about the rise of fascism in Europe.

By professional training and long years of teaching, I am knowledgeable about the historical slide by which seemingly vibrant democracies succumbed to authoritarian rule. Militarized federal troops are shooting indiscriminately into crowds of ordinary people in our country. We are on that slide.

It dawned on me when I was in the ER and had a chance to catch my breath (post tear gas): my government did this to me. My own government. I was not shot by a random person in the street. A federal law enforcement officer pulled a trigger that sent an impact munition into my head.

The federal troops in Portland, their presence and conduct opposed by elected Portland and Oregon officials, fueled rather than dampened civil unrest. They wore military camouflage uniforms that said "police" but didn't clearly indicate what agency they came from. Legal observers and activists reported difficulty discerning the difference between the federal troops and private right-wing militia units. This is no small concern. As the distinguished Yale historian Timothy Snyder, an expert on the rise of authoritarian regimes, said on MSNBC on the evening of July 25th:

"In a rule-of-law state, which is what we should be, you can tell the police from the civilians. When the police don't identify themselves, when the police don't wear insignia,

> when the police act as if they're above the law, then you've moved clearly into an authoritarian direction. It's the dark fantasy both in life and in literature of authoritarianism and totalitarianism that someone who you can't identify arrests you and takes you away in the middle of the night…This is something we would should be attending to."

Indications were that the federal Black-shirts sent to Portland were with U.S. Customs and Border Protection and brought up from the southern U.S. border. That made authoritarian sense. As Snyder explained to MSNBC's Rachel Maddow:

> "[Empires' authoritarian] violence [against their own citizens] starts at the borderland. People [gendarmes] can become accustomed to violence at the border. And then what an authoritarian regime does is it brings those people [gendarmes] back into the cities and uses them against protesters in the cities. People who are trained to think of Others as 'not like us,' as aliens, as foreigners are then told 'oh, well there happen to be people inland who are also not like us."

Sensing correctly that Immigrations and Customs Enforcement (ICE) operatives were also slated for deployment against homeland protesters, Snyder made a comparable point about how immigrant concentration camps (properly identified as such by Alexandria Ocasio-Cortez) provide "lawless" breeding grounds for authoritarian repression within authoritarian states:

> "A similar aspect here is the detention centers. We have this huge network of detention centers, which are basically lawless zones. Another historical pattern [in the development of authoritarian states] is that people who are trained in lawless zones such as detention centers or concentration camps are then released into cities later on and they behave the same way. They behave the way they've been trained."

The domestic paramilitaries and mercenaries strayed far beyond their ostensible legal mission of protecting federal facilities. According to a July 25th *New York Times* report:

> "After flooding the streets around the federal courthouse in Portland with tear gas during Friday's early morning hours, dozens of federal officers in camouflage and tactical gear stood in formation around the front of the building. Then, as one protester blared a soundtrack of "The Imperial March," the officers started advancing. Through the acrid haze, they continued to fire flash grenades and welt-inducing marble-size balls filled with caustic chemicals. They moved down Main Street and continued up the hill, where one of the agents announced over a loudspeaker: 'This is an unlawful assembly.'"

> "By the time the security forces halted their advance, the federal courthouse they had been sent to protect was out of sight—two blocks behind them. The aggressive incursion of federal officers into Portland has been stretching the legal limits of federal law enforcement, as agents with batons and riot gear range deep into the streets of a city whose leadership has made it clear they are not welcome."

Oregon's Democratic Senator Ron Wyden called the agents an "occupying army." House Speaker Nancy Pelosi called them "storm troopers."

Undeterred by the criticism, Trump justified the provocative, constitutionally dubious deployment of federal troops by claiming absurdly that Portland's "radical Left" mayor was "going to lose Portland."

Zakir Khan, a spokesperson for the Oregon chapter of the Council on American-Islamic Relations (CAIR), warned that the White House was using Portland as a test case. "They want to see what they can get away with before launching into other parts of the country," Khan told the *Washington Post*. Seattle Mayor Jenny Durkan told MSNBC at the end of July that Trump was "doing a dress rehearsal for martial law…Sending in federal forces, to take over police duties in city after city for political purposes," Durkan said, was "frightening and…making things worse."

Consistent with Khan's warning, Trump in late July announced "a surge of federal law enforcement into American communities plagued by violent crime." Trump claimed he would "immediately send surge federal law enforcement to Chicago. The FBI, ATF, DEA, U.S. Marshals Service, and Homeland Security will together be sending hundreds of skilled law enforcement officers to Chicago to help drive down violent crime." Trump, Mehdi Hasan said on MSNBC, "talked about Chicago the same way President George W. Bush talked about Fallujah, Iraq." (The two-thirds nonwhite city of Chicago had long served as Trump's top metropolitan "law and order" whipping boy. He had threatened Chicago with federal occupation throughout and indeed before his presidency.)

"We will put in 50,000, 60,000 people that really know what they're doing" into American cities, Trump told FOX News' leading white nationalist news anchor Sean Hannity. "And they're strong. They're tough. And we could solve these problems so fast." Shortly thereafter, Trump was threatening to send as many as 75,000 federal agents into American cities to quell crime.

The ostensible purpose of this "surge" was to stop the epidemic of shootings plaguing inner city neighborhoods across the U.S. In reality, the violence reflected a deadly combination: the sharp misery of the nation's urban Black communities, deeply exacerbated by the Trump virus (COVID-19), and the widespread availability of guns, enabled by Trump's allies in the Republican Party and the National Rifle Association. A serious effort to end violence in the poor Black communities of Chicago and other American cities would involve flooding disadvantaged neighborhoods with social and public health relief, not repression combined with serious gun control programs.

What Trump was actually trying to accomplish was to score points with his white Amerikaner "heartland" base and far-right bankrollers. The fascist, white-nationalist political playbook he operated from said that he was a "strong leader" ready to humiliate and discipline "radical left" and "liberal" Democratic Party elites atop largely Black and brown cities where supposedly unworthy non-white Others had purportedly been granted too much freedom. The images of urban confrontation and chaos were seen as Nixonian campaign commercial gold by Trump and his re-election team.

By mid-July if not before, the Trump campaign was using "urban nightmare" images of violence in his campaign ads—this while telling "suburban housewives" that the Democrats wanted to send angry Black and brown mobs out to destroy peaceful white suburbs. "They want to abolish the suburbs," Trump claimed. A Trump campaign commercial showed an older white suburban woman looking at terrifying pictures of urban protesters on her television while a voice-over of Hannity reported falsely that Democratic Party presidential nominee Joe Biden waned to "defund the police." A mysterious dark invader breaks into her house and presumably murders her in the commercial. As National Public Radio reported:

> President Trump has a message for suburban voters. And it's not a subtle one. "They want to destroy our suburbs," Trump recently warned in a call with supporters. "People have worked all their lives to get into a community, and now they're going to watch it go to hell," he said from the South Lawn of the White House....Trump has been issuing increasingly dire and outlandish warnings about what Democrats will do to the suburbs. He warns suburbanites will face rising crime and falling home values if they elect Joe Biden. The message: Be afraid, be very afraid.

To repeat one of Jason Stanley's key points, the demonization and fear of great multicultural cities is a consistent and recurrent theme in fascist politics.

When it came to the coronavirus this summer, Trump's position was that "it's up to the states." When it has come to repressing Black people and others in the nation's cities, Trump has been eager to flood the streets with federal agents of militarized, police-state repression.

Faced with Trump's use of federal paramilitary forces against protesters in Portland and his threatened coming attacks on other U.S. cities in mid-late July, leftish liberal commentators like *New York Times* columnist Michelle Goldberg, MSNBC's Chris Hayes, and MSNBC guest Medhi Hasan voiced the sadly controversial opinion that the Trump administration was now seriously and not just performatively "fascist." "Can we call it fascism yet?" the Times asked. "It's time," Hasan said on July 24th, to say "the F-word, fascism" in regard to Trump.[13]

Truth be told, it was time to do that at least four years before.

THE END OF THE AMERICAN EXPERIMENT

Behind the headlines provided by the fascistic Trumpian madness of June, Trump fired numerous departmental inspectors general for investigating matters that could have caused Trump embarrassment. He also fired Geoffrey Berman, the U.S. Attorney for the Southern District of New York as punishment for pursuing cases that caused Trump embarrassment: prosecuting and convicting Trump's former fixer, Michael Cohen; investigating the dealings of Trump lawyer Rudy Giuliani; looking into whether a bank with ties to Turkey's leader had violated Iran sanctions.

In early July, Trump's press secretary Kayleigh McEnany described a new book about Trump written by the president's professional psychologist niece Mary Trump as a "book of falsehoods" after admitting that she had yet to see the volume. Around the same time, Trump insanely fumed that he was a victim of "political persecution" when the U.S. Supreme Court ruled that his status as president did not grant him blanket immunity from the legal investigation of his financial records. Along the way, Trump continued his ongoing propaganda war against mail-in ballots, falsely claiming that they were extremely subject to fraud, in his determination to discredit the results of the November 2020 election if it does not go his way. He shocked what was left of the nation's constitutional sensibilities by commuting the federal prison sentence of his longtime far-right political ally and trickster Roger Stone, who was convicted for lying to Congress in order to protect Trump and his campaign. It was a blatant abuse of the president's pardon power—a "transparent effort to convince his supporters that his access to power should not be constrained by his oath to uphold the Constitution," as law professor Joyce White Vance observed.

Also sending an authoritarian chill down the spine of civil libertarians was the two-week re-incarceration of Michael Cohen in July of 2020. In 2018, Cohen had pleaded guilty to a federal judge of financial and campaign finance crimes and lying to Congress about his involvement in an effort to build a "Trump Tower" in Moscow during the 2016 campaign. On May 21, 2020, Cohen had been released from federal prison early to serve the rest of his sentence under house arrest because of concerns regarding COVID-19. But Trump's Attorney General William Barr ordered him back into federal custody after Cohen refused to consent to conditions that banned him from communicating with the media. Cohen filed suit alleging that his re-arrest was an attempt to prevent him from releasing a tell-all book about Donald Trump. On July 23 a federal judge agreed, ordered that he be returned to home confinement. Manhattan federal judge Alvin Hellerstein found that Cohen's re-imprisonment was a "retaliatory" effort to punish Cohen for trying "to exercise his first amendment rights to publish a book and to discuss anything about the book or anything else he wants on social media and with others."

The title of Mary Trump's book was *Too Much and Never Enough: How My Family Created the World's Most Dangerous Man.* To nobody's surprise, Ms. Trump revealed that the president is a sick and sadistic man incapable of human empathy, that he hired someone to take his SAT exam, and that he grew up under the abusive control of a domineering father while spouting racist, antisemitic, sexist, and homophobic rhetoric. More alarming perhaps was Ms. Trump's warning on cable news that her uncle's re-election would be "the end of the American experiment." By the "American experiment," Ms. Trump meant "democracy"—or (to use language she would likely avoid) what's left of it under the longstanding rule of the nation's unelected and interrelated dictatorships of money and empire.

In cold defiance of constitutional free speech principles, the Trump administration fought to prevent both the publication of Ms. Trump's book and to block her from speaking about the book and the president in public. Along with former Trump National Security Adviser John Bolton's White House memoir, *The Room Where it Happened*, released in late June, it was the second book the Trump administration had tried to ban from the marketplace last summer.

There is good reason to wonder if Trump will accept an Electoral College count that does not go his way next November, and good reason to hope that the nation's military command is ready and willing to force his removal if he is defeated. Trump refusing to leave and having to be escorted out of the White House by a military that may not wish to perform this duty, while Trump, his Attorney General, and his party claim vote fraud, is an entirely realistic scenario for which Americans would do well to prepare. The president has long been seeding the narrative that he cannot be fairly or legally removed from office and that no election won by his opponent could be legitimate. His diatribes concerning alleged voter fraud have always had at their core the preposterous notion that it is impossible for him to rightfully lose the upcoming election.

"Given my experience working for Mr. Trump," Trump's long-time personal attorney and "fixer" Michael Cohen told Congress last year, "I fear that if he loses the election in 2020, there will never be a peaceful transition of power." Earlier this year, the conservative American Enterprise Institute scholar Norman Ornstein and the Trump official "Anonymous" warned that the tyrant Trump may not honor the outcome of an election result that doesn't go his way. "Members of Congress, governors, and state legislators, leaders in civil society, lawyers, law enforcement figures, and the military need," Ornstein said, "to be thinking about how they might respond."

Consistent with Cohen, Ornstein, and Anonymous's warnings, Trump repeatedly launched the unproven charge that the mass mail-in ballots required by the pandemic would be subject to fraud. He used this as a pretext to float on Twitter the suggestion that the 2020 elections might have to be "delayed." This alarming suggestion led even the founder of the right-wing Federalist Society to Tweet about Trump's "fascistic" essence. It provoked a number of liberal responses pointing out that Trump had no power to suspend an election under the Constitution. The responses seemed not to know or to forget that Trump had been spending his entire presidency blowing through one constitutional check and balance after another. Whatever the possibilities of suspension (not to be ruled out in the context of some kind of declared state of emergency), it was already clear as day that Trump and his party were doing everything they could to inhibit, cripple, and de-legitimize a 2020 election that polls strongly forecast them to lose.

Particularly ominous were reports that Trump's recently appointed Postmaster General Louis DeJoy, a wealthy businessman and leading Trump fundraiser, was implementing policies leading to major backlogs in mail delivery. Fear that the problem could continue through November and affect the election were reinforced by an internal US Post Service report warning that nearly half the states were not providing adequate time for workers to deliver ballots ahead of the election. Several of the states potentially affected are battleground ones that will determine if Donald Trump or Joe Biden is the next president and it is big, heavily Democratic cities will likely be most impacted. One does not have to be a paranoid-style conspiratorialist to see a real menace to electoral democracy, or what's left of it, in the United States this fall.

Apocalypse, anyone?

"THE MOST DANGEROUS CRIMINAL IN HUMAN HISTORY"

Depressingly enough, racist neofascism and reckless pandemic-fanning may not be the most grave and apocalyptic menaces posed by Trump and Trumpism. What has most marked Trump as what the great public intellectual Noam Chomsky calls "the most dangerous criminal in human history" is the current president's consistent, all-out war on environmental regulation and his fierce climate-denialist determination to accelerate the process of turning the entire planet into a giant greenhouse gas chamber. Along the way, Trump has quietly increased the threat of nuclear war. As Chomsky explained last February:

> Hitler['s] goal was to rid the German-run world of Jews, Roma, homosexuals and other "deviants," along with tens of millions of Slav "Untermenschen." *But Hitler was not dedicated with fervor to destroying the prospects of organized human life on Earth in the not-distant future (along with millions of other species). Trump is...*He devotes every effort to accelerating the race to [environmental] catastrophe, trailed by such lesser lights as [fellow climate-deniers] Brazil's Jair Bolsonaro and Australia's Scott Morrison....Every day brings new forebodings...It has now been confirmed, as suspected, that ..."a layer of relatively warmer ocean water, which circles Antarctica below the colder surface layer, ha[s] moved closer to shore and begun to eat away at the glaciers themselves, affecting West Antarctica in particular"...This is only one of the likely irreversible tipping points that may be reached if "the Chosen One," as he modestly describes himself, *is granted another four years to carry out his project of global destruction.*

> ... in recent days, the Chosen One has issued executive orders *ridding the country of the plague of regulations that protect children from mercury poisoning and preserve the country's water supplies and lands,* along with other impediments

to further enrichment of Trump's primary constituency, extreme wealth and corporate power.

On the side, he has been casually proceeding to *dismantle the last vestiges of the arms control regime that has provided some limited degree of security from terminal nuclear war*, eliciting cheers from the military industry. [Emphasis added]

The eco-exterminist attitude of the Trump administration was nicely epitomized in May of 2019, when Trump's Interior Secretary David Bernhardt told a House Democrat "I haven't lost any sleep over" over reports that carbon's atmospheric presence has reached 415 parts per million, the highest level in more than 800,000 years. Bernhardt was a longtime energy industry and agribusiness lobbyist charged, of all things, with the federal management and protection of the nation's public lands and natural resources.

Consistent with Chomsky's additional ("on the side") warning about nuclear escalation, the *Washington Post* reported that senior Trump administration officials met in mid-May of 2020 to illegally ignore the 1996 Comprehensive Test Ban Treaty by resuming atmospheric nuclear tests. In a late June follow-up, the arch-reactionary and arch-Trumpist U.S. Senator Tom Cotton (R-AR) introduced an amendment to the 2021 National Defense Authorization Act (NDAA) that would give the Trump administration "no less than $10 million" to conduct a nuclear weapons test. The amendment passed by a vote along partisan lines and is under debate as this book goes to press.

In February of 2020, for what it's worth, *Defense News* reported that "a new nuclear warhead requested, designed and produced under the Trump administration, has been deployed aboard a nuclear submarine." The new and highly provocative weapon, the W76-2, is a "a low-yield variant of the nuclear warhead traditionally used on the Trident missile." Antiproliferation experts raised concerns dismissed by Trump's Pentagon: "having a low-yield and high-yield warhead launched on the same submarine-launched missile creates a situation where an adversary doesn't know which system is being used and therefore reacts as if the larger warhead has been launched." In short, the W76-2 increases the chances for an *apocalyptic* global nuclear war.

If historians still exist in future decades, some of them may be struck by how Donald Trump's Democratic Party critics and their many media allies ignored these existential threats as they obsessed for nearly three years over the Trump's real and/ or alleged connections to Russia and to Russian oligarchs and to their purported roles in "rigging" the 2016 election. While they said comparatively little about his dedicated efforts to speed humanity's march towards extinction in service to American corporate polluters, they spent hundreds of hours and countless miles of newsprint shrilly lamenting alleged Russian election interference on behalf of Trump. Meanwhile, the Trump administration was quietly speeding up the end of history with a broad sweep of horrific (anti-) environmental policies and practices.

NO BATON

Despite the rhetoric, there was no "baton" of freedom, democracy, and justice—much less ecological sanity—handed off from Obama to Trump on January 20, 2017. Obama didn't have one to pass on in the first place, but even if he did, the apocalyptic instinctual fascist and eco-exterminist Trump was not remotely interested in running such a relay. Obama knew this, but kept his understanding "strategically" private, consistent with his longstanding "deeply conservative" embrace of reigning domestic and imperial institutions and ideologies. His all-too accurate pre-election understanding of Trump as a "fascist," born-out by subsequent events, has remained private in the post-2016 years, reflecting perhaps Obama's understanding that his own presidency helped bring "the most dangerous criminal in human history" to power in the first place, as we shall see in this book's third's chapter.

Obama's pattern of public silence would hold for the next three plus years. As the nation plunged deeper into despair and rage, right up to the point where this book stops—in the disease and violence-plagued summer of 2020—the highly (if unjustly) popular former president had remarkably little serious to directly say about it all, all things considered. When he did "speak up," his remarks would be depressingly tepid, milquetoast, and indirect, carefully avoiding Trump's name along with the overriding issues of Trump's fascism and eco-cidalism. Obama's most direct and aggressive remarks would be wedded to the nation's savagely narrow and time-staggered election cycle, consistent with Obama's deeply held faith in notion that, in the late radical historian Howard Zinn's words, "the most important act a citizen can engage in is to go to the polls and choose of the two mediocrities who have already been chosen for you."

Along the way, as the nation fell ever deeper into the "apocalypse" he said wasn't happening after the last election, former president Obama has enjoyed personal entrance to the economic oligarchy, tasting the lifestyle benefits of wealth and celebrity while cashing in (the subject of this book's fourth chapter) on his many years of service to the corporate and financial elite. He has also dedicated time and energy and his extreme popularity to (as we shall see in this book's fifth chapter) promoting largely behind the scenes the presidential candidacy of a true corporate Democratic "mediocrity" if ever there was one: Joe Biden, a right-wing corporatist and imperialist who owes much of his strange and disturbing presence on the national stage to America's 44th president.

ENDNOTES

1. I take this phrase from historian Margaret George's classic study of British foreign policymakers who appeased the rise of Nazi Germany. See M. George, *The Hollow Men: An Examination of British Foreign Policy, 1933–39* (London: Frewin, 1967). See also my review of David Garrow's epic biography of Obama: Paul Street, "Obama: a Hollow Man Filled With Ruling Class Ideas,"

Counterpunch, June 7, 2017, https://www.counterpunch.org/2017/06/02/obama-a-hollow-man-filled-with-ruling-class-ideas/

2   David Remnick, "Obama Reckons with a Trump Presidency," *The New Yorker*, November 18, 2016.

3. If sincerely meant, Obama's post-election call for Democrats and others to "go forward with a presumption of good faith in our fellow citizens" was extremely naïve. Trump's largely petit-bourgeois and overwhelmingly white base is chillingly consistent with the sociopolitical profile of fascist and other reactionary populist and ethno-nationalist movements past and present. The most sophisticated and statistically astute analysis of the 2016 Trump electorate produced so far has been crafted by political sociologists David Norman Smith and Eric Hanley. In an article published in *Critical Sociology* in March of 2018, Smith and Hanley found that the white Trump base was differentiated from white non-Trump voters not by class or other "demographic" factors (including income, age, gender and the alleged class identifier of education) but by eight key attitudes and values: identification as "conservative;" support for "domineering leaders;" Christian fundamentalism; prejudice against immigrants; prejudice against blacks; prejudice against Muslims; prejudice against women; a sense of pessimism about the economy. Strong Trump supporters scored particularly high on support for domineering leaders, fundamentalism, opposition to immigrants and economic pessimism. They were particularly prone to support authoritarian leaders who promised to respond punitively to minorities perceived as "line-cutters"—"undeserving" others who were allegedly getting ahead of traditional white Americans in the procurement of jobs and government benefits—and to the supposed liberal "rotten apples" who were purportedly allowing these "line-cutters" to advance ahead of traditional white American males. Support for politically authoritarian leaders and a sense of intolerance regarding racial, ethnic and gender differences are two sides of the same Trumpian coin. The basic desire animating Trump's base is "the defiant wish for a domineering and impolitic leader" linked to "the wish for a reversal of what his base perceives as an inverted moral and racial order."

4. https://thehill.com/blogs/blog-briefing-room/news/479947-kaine-obama-called-trump-a-fascist-during-2016-campaign. When apprised of Obama's comment, Hillary Clinton said "I echo that sentiment… that's really—the weight of our responsibility is so huge."

5. Adam Gopnik, "Going There With Donald Trump," *The New Yorker*, May 11, 2016.

6. Curt Guyette, "Is Trump a Fascist? The F-Word," *Detroit Metro Times*, September 11, 2019, https://www.metrotimes.com/detroit/is-trump-a-fascist/Content?oid=22617920&fbclid=IwAR0et8NBmnvDiji9ymmWRqmS4iW-puEsy2spxe8JO32y2oRqqWirYbJ20VIM

7. John Haltiwanger, "Trump still believes coronavirus will 'just disappear' as the US nears 130,000 reported deaths," *Business Insider,* July 1, 2020, https://www. businessinsider.com/trump-still-believes-coronavirus-will-just-disappear-as-cases-rise-2020-7

8. Behrmann, Savannah, " 'Science Should Not Stand in the Way' of Schools Reopening, White House Press Secretary Kayleigh McEnany Says," *USA Today*, July 17, 2020, https://news.yahoo.com/science-not-stand-way-schools-221937989.html?soc_src=community&soc_trk=fb

9. Diamond, Dan; Lippman, Daniel; Cook, Nancy, "Trump Team Launches a Sweeping Loyalty Test to Shore up Its Defenses," *POLITICO,* July 15, 2020, https://www.politico.com/news/2020/07/15/trump-appointees-loyalty-inter-views-364616?fbclid=IwAR0QIWx6sDhaMt8JnidLBnRbIUi_FAWECBa_lriLF-CkwlxmXLGd753yUtFM

10. Baker, Peter; Haberman, Maggie; Rogers, Katie; Kanno-Youngs, Zolan; Benner, Katie; Willis, Haley; Triebert, Christiaan; Botti, David (June 2, 2020). "How Trump's Idea for a Photo Op Led to Havoc in a Park". *The New York Times.* Archived from the original on June 6, 2020

11. Ignatius, David. "How Trump came to the brink of deploying active-duty troops in Washington," *Washington Post.* Retrieved June 7, 2020

12. Gessen, Masha. "Donald Trump's Fascist Performance," *The New Yorker,* June 3, 2020. https://www.newyorker.com/news/our-columnists/donald-trumps-fas-cist-performance

13. Hasan, Mehdi, "It's Time We Use the F-Word: Fascism," MSNBC, July 24, 2020, https://www.msnbc.com/all-in/watch/mehdi-hasan-it-s-time-we-use-the-f-wo rd-fascism-88251973935?fbclid=IwAR08-PBnLnwgjpuf44YX2OVVX5CQxUk-kli6UTBeztN1rPFy7m_wftecWtoE

CHAPTER TWO
Where's Obama?

> The former president, who did not mention President
> Donald Trump by name, has generally shied away from
> weighing in on politics or criticizing his successor since
> leaving office…
> —*POLITICO*, May 16, 2020

> There's a tricky balance here. As much as former president
> Obama has an enormous microphone and people still
> look to hear what he has to say, he also, especially at a
> time of global crisis, *does not want to create a moment that's
> perceived as political.*
> —Jen Psaki, a former communications director in the
> Obama'White House, March 31, 2020.

> When his staff brings him ideas, issues, outrages that he
> might address, Obama always asks a simple question: "To
> what end?" More often than not, he stays mum.
> —Ryan Lizza, "Waiting for Obama," *POLITICO,* November
> 26, 2019

> Where the hell is Barack Obama? …I'm sick of Barack
> Obama staying above the fray while that fray is swallowing
> us whole. It's infuriating.
> —Drew Magarty, April 14, 2020

WHACK-A-MOLE: APOCALYPSE NOW

Neither his private understanding of Trump's fascism nor
whatever he thought or knew about Trump's strange relationship
with Russia prevented Obama from leaving his successor a letter
in which he reminded Trump that "we are just temporary occu-
pants of this office. That makes us guardians of those democratic
institutions and traditions—like rule of law, separation of powers,
equal protection and civil liberties—that our forebears fought
and bled for. Regardless of the push and pull of daily politics, it's

up to us to leave those instruments of our democracy at least as strong as we found them."

It is hard not to laugh while reading those words in light of Trump's record so far (not that Obama lived up those shining words himself—he didn't). Journalists and academics have found it difficult to keep up with Trump's crimes. Tracking Trump's record of transgressions is like playing a game of whack-a-mole: just when you think have a handle on his abuses, you discover one, two, and three or more. The Leadership Conference on Civil and Human Rights (LCHR) has compiled a list[1] of the Trump administration's rolling blitzkrieg of real, proposed, and attempted human and civil rights rollbacks during Trump's first three years in office. The catalogue has two hundred entries, a chilling testament to the Trump team's undying hostility to Black civil rights; racial, ethnic, and gender equality and diversity; immigrant rights; women's rights; consumer protections; labor and worker rights; gay and transgender rights; the poor and antipoverty programs; welfare rights; student rights.

A clever and comprehensive online registry is titled "Lest We Forget: A Catalogue of Trump's Worst Cruelties, Collusions, Corruptions, and Crimes." The catalog begins in February of 2011 and contains 759 transgressions, all but 42 of which occurred on or since the day Trump became president, through the end of May 2020. To help readers wade through the crime record, the catalogue's compilers used a color-coded "Atrocity Key," separately marking cases of corruption, racism, xenophobia, assaults on the environment, and more.[2]

I have compiled my own online appendix to this book to be posted on my website, www.paulstreet.org, under the title "Shock and Awe: This Happened in Trump's First and Hopefully Only Term." This document is available through a simple Google search of my name and the appendix's title. It will contain an abbreviated, bullet-pointed, and semi-chronological list of Trump's most egregious transgressions from his first day in office through August of 2020. The list was created to avoid burdening the flow of the present volume's narrative. I recommend consulting it at some point while reading this book. Trump's criminal record as president must be seen in total to be believed.

The nonstop attack is, the anti-fascist activist Jay Becker writes, "part of the fascist playbook, be on the constant offensive, exhaust your adversaries. One feature that distinguishes it from 'good old fashioned' authoritarians."

NORMS HONORED AND SMASHED

Where has Obama been as Trump has repeatedly validated the forty-fourth president's private description of his successor as a "fascist" and used the world's most powerful office to act in accord with Noam Chomsky's description of him as "the most dangerous criminal in human history"? What has he had to say as the demented fascistic oligarch Trump has continued his regular, even obsessive, transparently racialized habit of trashing everything Obama, attacking all of Obama's "signature" policies as well as many lesser-known ones, taunting his predecessor with absurdly false charges, and repeatedly blaming Obama for problems largely of Trump's own making?

It's been no small dilemma for Obama. The longstanding convention holding that ex-U.S. presidents say little about the performance and politics of their successors is consistent both with Obama's conservative psychological and ideological discomfort with conflict and with his longstanding faith in accommodation across racial, ethnic, socioeconomic, and party lines. The norm is a good match for Barack "No Drama Obama's" reputation for "staying cool," avoiding conflict and outward expressions of strong emotion.

But the indecent beast Trump is nothing if not a dramatic norm-smasher. He's a viciously racist, sexist, and fascistic eco-exterminist menace to life on Earth who has broken numerous pre-existing conventions on presidential behavior, including the expectation not to mercilessly and repeatedly trash one's predecessor. In fact, Trump has been obsessed with Obama, maniacally blaming the forty-fourth president for the challenges and shortcomings that have marked Trump's tenure while feverishly comparing his record to Obama in an unconcealed bid to out-compete and denigrate the previous chief executive—even, indeed, to erase Obama from the historical record. If ever a sitting president has provided a justifiable basis for an ex-president—especially a highly popular and influential one still in his intellectual prime—to break with the conservative norms on how an ex-president should behave, Trump has made the case. The forty-fifth U.S. President has represented a dramatic threat to democracy, decency, and life itself—a challenge to emotionally and politically neutral calm if ever we've seen one in the White House.

Obama, predictably, has mostly decided not to step up. His responses to the fascistic horror and personalized, racialized onslaught have been excruciatingly sparse, mild, indirect, careful, and weak, with only occasional and partial exceptions linked to Obama's foundational attachment to the nation's savagely time-staggered election cycle. His deeply conservative pro-corporate and imperial world view (formulated well before his presidency, as we shall see in this book's final chapter) has colored his tepid rejoinders, echoing the positions he took during his presidency and earlier political career.

Notably, Obama's many fans in the officially neutral corporate media have tended to significantly oversell the extent to which Obama has challenged the ongoing disparagement and dismantlement of his administration's policies and the broader horror of Trump. Political reporters, commentators, and talking heads, and pundits have been excessively eager to declare Obama's often vacuous responses as clarion calls for what the media operatives fashion as serious opposition and resistance.

There is one way in which Obama has broken with long-established norms for behavior on the part of ex-presidents, however.

As we shall see in the fourth chapter, he has spent no small time hobnobbing with celebrities and enjoying the lifestyles of the rich and the famous while climbing into the nation's opulent economic aristocracy. It appears he is collecting a deferred payment for his many years of dutiful service to the nation's unelected dictatorship in office, including his eight years in the most powerful position on the planet. Obama's big and unseemly cash-in has contrasted curiously but perhaps appropriately with his cautious and conservative, norm-honoring response to Trump's norm-smashing presidency.

"WHERE I THINK OUR CORE VALUES ARE AT STAKE"

Shortly before leaving office, the famously voluble Barack Obama said there were issues on which he would speak out as a private citizen. "There's a difference," Obama told reporters in his final presidential press conference, "between that normal functioning of politics and certain issues or certain moments where I think our core values may be at stake."[3]

Obama has not felt compelled to say much at all about any but a relatively tiny number of Trump's transgressions, a frightening number of which have gone far beyond the previously understood "normal functioning of politics." Even when Trump's malignant and reckless lunacy has been aimed straight at Obama and his legacy, moreover, Obama's responses have been few and far between, showing a deep reluctance to engage, especially when election dates are distant. When the Muhammad Ali fan *has* shown some willingness to the publicly step into the ring, he has tended to do so only when Trump's awfulness is simply too terrible to ignore, when Obama's own top "signature" policies have been attacked or dismantled, or when elections draw near.

Indeed, Obama's response has for the most part been cringingly cautious and deeply conservative. He has been absurdly loath to mention Trump by name, so much so that *The New York Times* could report the following three years and six months into Trump's nightmare presidency: "Mr. Obama [is]…so determined to avoid uttering the new president's name that one aide jokingly suggest[s] they refer to him as 'He-Who-Must-Not-Be-Named'—Harry Potter's archenemy, Lord Voldemort."[4] At the same time, Obama has been reluctant to recommend forceful public protest of Trump and Trumpism beyond electoral support for corporate and imperial Democrats. He has been unwilling to identify Trump and/or Trumpism as fascist, racist, nativist, sexist, or eco-exterminist. He has of course never acknowledged his own responsibility for helping birth the Trumpenstein, much less for passing on deadly authoritarian and imperial tools and precedents to his lethal successor, the most dangerous criminal in human history.

THE PRESIDENT DISAGREES

Take Trump's original Muslim travel ban, validated a year and half later by the U.S. Supreme Court. Obama personally said nothing about this outrage in public, though his official spokesman Kevin Lewis did issue this carefully worded statement while tens of thousands of Americans protested the measure at U.S. airports:

> Former president Obama is heartened by the level of [citizen] engagement…In his final official speech as President, he spoke about the important role of citizen[s] and how all Americans have a responsibility to be the guardians of our democracy…Citizens exercising their Constitutional right to assemble, organize and have their voices heard by their elected officials is exactly what we expect to see when American values are at stake…With regard to comparisons to President Obama's foreign policy decisions, as we've heard before, the President fundamentally disagrees with the notion of discriminating against individuals because of their faith or religion.[5]

KIDS IN CAGES: HELLO OBAMA?

What about the Trump administration's vicious immigrant policy of family separation, sold to the public as a "zero tolerance" approach to deter illegal immigration? From the spring of 2017 through the fall of 2019, Trump's immigration officers separated children from parents or guardians with whom they had entered the US at the U.S.-Mexico border. The adults were incarcerated in federal jails while the children were placed under the supervision of the US Department of Health and Human Services. The policy included no measures to reunite the families.

Separated families and kids in cages? Obama has said nothing, or close to nothing, about these harsh detention and deportation policies, which included the placing of Mexican and Central American children literally in cages. Obama remained "above it all," staying silent even as a high-profile partisan slugfest arose over what Representative Alexandria Ocasio-Cortez called Trump's "concentration camps" and as Trump claimed that his scandalous policy had actually been initiated by Obama. Obama's silence may have reflected the unpleasant fact that his administration also subjected migrants to horrific conditions in federal detention centers, detaining them in appalling circumstances, though with few if any family separations.

CHARLOTTESVILLE? HELLO?

What about Trump's shocking response to the racist "Unite the Right" rally Charlottesville, Virginia in August 2017, when the 45th President of the United States said that the white supremacists who chanted "Blood and Soil" and "Jews Will Not Replace Us" included "some very fine people" and absurdly blamed "the alt-Left" for fascist violence (including the murder of female counter-protester Heather Heyer)? It was one of Trump's signature neofascist moments and it produced another firestorm of denunciation from politicians, activists, and media. One might have expected that the nation's first Black president would have been among those sounding the alarm over the current president equating Nazis with democratic protesters. But Obama didn't rise to the occasion. The former leader of the "free" world responded with a tepid Tweet, setting a new record for the most liked Tweet of all time with the following comment: "No one is born hating another person because of the color of his skin, or his background, or his religion. People must learn to hate, and if they can learn to hate, they can be taught to love, for love comes more naturally to the human heart than its opposite." That was it. Beyond this indirect criticism, Obama remained tongue-tied about Trump's disturbing comments. He made no mention of Trump or the explicitly fascist and racist nature of the Charlottesville marchers. He made no reference to the young woman who was murdered by a white supremacist in Charlottesville or to Trump's sickening suggestion of moral equivalence between the white supremacists and the people who counter-protested in the name of civil rights, social justice, and racial equality. Obama's comments were restricted to cyberspace, unaccompanied by any other written or spoken comments in the public sphere.

SHITHOLE COUNTRIES? A NOT-SO-STERN WARNING FOR THE COMMANDER-IN-CHIEF

How about when Trump referred to Black Haiti and Black African nations as "shithole countries" in January of 2018, adding his wish that the U.S. would get immigrants not from these Black nations but rather from white countries like "Norway"? In an amusing example of the corporate media's desire to portray Obama as having fought back against Trump, CNN claimed that Obama had responded to this insult with "a stern warning for the current commander in chief." The "warning" CNN referenced came out of a January 15th Netflix interview with David Letterman, a discussion in which Obama made no direct or explicit reference to Trump or Trump's racist comment. "One of the things that Michelle figured out, in some ways faster than I did," Obama told Letterman, "was part of your ability to lead the country doesn't have to do with legislation, doesn't have to do with regulations, it has to do with shaping attitudes, shaping culture, increasing awareness."[6] This was harmless and anodyne discourse with little real world relevance. Again, a former president of "hope" and "change" offered no stinging rebuke to Trump's blatant racist nationalism. Obama failed as usual to mention Trump by name and seemed to absurdly understand Trump as someone who wanted to increase cultural sensitivity and inclusion.

"OBAMA FINALLY SPEAKS OUT ON TRUMP"

Obama did finally tackle Trump's response to Charlottesville in a speech more than one year later (!), on the eve of the 2018 mid-term Congressional elections. Halfway through an hour-long address at the University of Illinois at Urbana-Champaign, Obama said this:

> It shouldn't be Democratic or Republican to say we don't target certain groups of people based on what they look like or how they pray. We are Americans. We're supposed to stand up to bullies—not follow them. We're supposed to stand up to discrimination, and we're sure as heck supposed to stand up clearly and unequivocally to Nazi sympathizers. How hard can that be? Saying that Nazis are bad?

That was it. In its coverage of Obama's Urbana speech, the leading centrist political journal and website *The Hill* said that "since leaving office last year, Obama has offered only occasional, veiled criticisms of Trump. His remarks on Friday marked *the first time he went after the president by name.*"[7] [Emphasis added.]

This was quite an exaggeration. Going through a transcript of the hour-long speech, one can find only two named references to Trump and neither of them could seriously have been considered "going after the president":

> "It did not start with Donald Trump. He is a symptom, not the cause. He's just capitalizing on resentments that politicians have been fanning for years."

> "Because in the end, the threat to our democracy *does not just come from Donald Trump* or the current batch of Republicans in Congress or the Koch brothers and their lobbyists or too much compromise by Democrats or Russian hacking."[8]

Not only did neither of these two named references "go after" Trump. Both downplayed the relevance of the menace posed by Trump, folding the fascist president into the broader category of the Republican Party and its financial sponsors and allies.

POLITICO put up a video of the speech under the title, "Obama Finally Speaks Out On Trump."[9] It was a curious spin on a speech in which Obama could bring himself to mention Trump just twice and then only indirectly, a speech that could criticize Trump's outrageous Charlottesville response only in oblique fashion and a full year after the outrage. Even more absurd was the headline and prefatory commentary the widely read news website *Vox* gave to a transcript of Obama's Urbana speech:

> *Read the Transcript of Obama's Fiery Anti-Trump Speech.*

> Barack Obama is *done holding back*. The former president unloaded on President Trump—by name—and Republicans in Congress during a blistering speech at the University of Illinois Urbana-Champaign on Friday, urging students in the audience to vote in an election he called a turning point. [Emphasis added.]

MAYBE WE CAN CHANGE THEIR MINDS

Obama's oversold Urbana oration was consistent with a speech he gave in honor of Nelson Mandela in mid-July of 2018 in South Africa, his first major address since leaving office. In Johannesburg, Obama held forth on threats to "democracy as we know it, posed" by "right-wing populism" and "authoritarian rulers" without once mentioning Trump by name, without referencing fascism, and without giving even remotely appropriate attention to the deep-seated racism and ethno-centrism that provided the social and electoral foundation for the rise of twenty-first century "reactionary populists" like Trump, Victor Orban, Vladimir Putin, Narendra Modi, Marine Le Pen, and Jair Bolsonaro. As political commentator Zack Beauchamp observed, Obama's ninety-minute address was marred by one of his trademark defects: an unwillingness to name and confront evil and an over-eagerness to understand and accommodate the racist and nativist right:

> The speech …suffers from a characteristic Obama flaw: *over-generosity toward his political opponents.* The former president gives too much leeway to the legitimate grievances of right-wing populists, particularly overemphasizing the role of economic grievances in their rise and underplaying how committed these groups' supporters are to bigotry and xenophobia. The result is a speech that advocates trying to change the minds of many people whose minds are most likely unchangeable.

> …*Obama never once uttered the word "Trump" in the speech, but the president looms over it like the lettering on one of his hotels.*…

> …the evidence overwhelmingly suggests that the backlash Obama is concerned with reflects cultural resentments and prejudice. White Westerners are flocking to anti-immigrant and racially hostile parties because they feel that their status, their privilege, is threatened. It's less that economic struggles are making people racist, and more that developments that threaten white privilege—such as large-scale nonwhite immigration and the election of one Barack Obama—has sparked a racist backlash.

> Obama shies away from this diagnosis of the problem, seemingly because he wants to see the best in people. "Democracy demands that we're able also to get inside the reality of people who are different than us so we can understand their point of view," he says. "Maybe we can

> change their minds, but maybe they'll change ours." At the end of the speech, he suggests that this idea—people can be persuaded not to hate—should become the cornerstone of our politics.

> [But] Today's backlash politics isn't being pioneered by people ignorant of the ideals of 20th-century liberalism; it's coming from people who are steeped in them, and choose to center their ideal political movements on tearing down those ideals.

> ....But Obama's politics of compromise isn't enough in a moment that calls for a politics of combat.[10] [Emphasis added.]

The fact that Obama's politics continued to revolve around "compromise" spoke volumes about the former president's level of concern over his successor's clear determination to reshape the U.S. political landscape in terrible and unprecedented ways.

Obama's South Africa speech bemoaned authoritarian leaders' "denial of facts" without mentioning Trump by name and without mentioning that an assault on truth and objectivity is one of the hallmark characteristics of fascist politics. "Unfortunately," Obama said, "too much of politics today seems to reject the very concept of objective truth. *People* just make stuff up. We see the utter loss of shame among *political leaders* where they're caught in a lie and they just double down and lie some more. The denial of facts runs counter to democracy."

"People" and "political leaders" like the unnamed Trump, who was lying and otherwise misrepresenting reality at least ten times per day, according to careful estimates at the time? Obama seemed unwilling to warn the world about what the lying was intended to accomplish—the advance of authoritarian and nationalist rule—and the sort of nation and world Trump and his neofascist cohorts hoped to create.

As Vann R. Newkirk II, a young Black *Atlantic* correspondent, wrote, Obama's "inadequate" speech in South Africa showed that the former president "still doesn't understand Trump or the forces that elected him." The former president's "praise of a global, liberal, market-based economic framework in a speech that essentially asked people to be decent and act in good faith" failed to remotely grasp the depth of what Americans and others were facing in the form of Trumpism and other forms of neo-fascistic ethno-nationalism around the world. By Newkirk II's eloquent account, Obama's Johannesburg oration continued the former president's ongoing patten of failing to step up against the apocalyptic menace of Trump and Trumpism, and indeed of failing to even name the danger:

> Barack Obama doesn't often mention Donald Trump. More than anything else, that has been a constant in his random assortment of public appearances and statements since he left the White House. Even when he has occasionally answered the call from Americans to show leadership during a Trumpian scandal or crisis, Obama has preferred magnanimity, issuing statements exhorting his countrymen to soldier on and praising the goodness of the institutions they must lean on to do so.[11]

As Newkirk II might have added, it was tellingly significant that Obama's August 2018 speech, his strongest statement on right-wing politics since leaving office, was delivered in a foreign country.

DON'T SAY HIS (TRUMP'S) NAME

"Politicians Just Blatantly Lying"

Obama's fans can cite a speech or two where Obama has seemed to take down his guard and go after the sitting president a bit more assertively than usual. In Milwaukee in October of 2018, Obama gave what one reporter called a "fiery speech" on behalf of Democrats in the mid-term Congressional elections. Obama lit into "politicians [for] just blatantly, repeatedly, baldly, shamelessly, lying." Obama accused "politicians" of "making stuff up. Calling up, down. Calling black, white. That's what your governor is doing with [his campaign] ads, just making stuff up," Obama said, referring to Governor Scott Walker and his assertions that he wanted to protect health care for those with pre-existing conditions.

Obama's salvos were only directed at a Republican governor. Of course Obama could have said the same thing about his successor in the White House, who the *Washington Post* found to have made 19,126 false statements during his first 1,226 days[12] (three and one third years)—sixteen false statements per day!— and who also claimed to want to protect health insurance for people with pre-existing conditions while actively trying to do precisely the opposite. But Obama refused to make the leap. "The speech was one of Obama's sharpest and most direct criticism of Trump's presidency," reported the Associated Press's Ivan Moreno, "although"—no small qualification!—"the *former president was careful to never mention Trump by name*" (emphasis added). "Obama," Moreno exulted, "cited a recent Trump comment that he would pass a tax cut before the November election. Obama then told the crowd in a Milwaukee high school gymnasium that 'Congress isn't even in session! He just makes it up!'" Here Obama highlighted one of Trump's most irrelevant misrepresentations.

In Detroit the next day, Obama got a bit more fired up before a largely Black audience. "The character of our country is on the ballot," he roared. "While he rarely addressed Trump by name," the *Detroit News* reported, "Obama repeatedly criticized his bombastic successor while lamenting what he called a 'cynical' politics of division." Further:

> He accused Republicans of trying to distract voters from critical issues. Instead of talking about Flint water, infrastructure or health care, Trump is trying to fire up his base by talking about "impoverished refugees 1,000 miles away," he said, referencing the Honduran migrant caravan the Republican president has bemoaned.

And Obama repeatedly criticized "lies" coming out of Washington, D.C., arguing that telling the truth should be something that Democrats and Republicans should agree on.

"When words stop meaning anything, when truth doesn't matter, when people can just make up facts, then democracy, it doesn't work," Obama said. "There's no accountability."

That was it—that was Obama's "fiery" attack on the fascist—mostly unnamed and never called what Obama knew him and his party to be (white-nationalist and neofascist)—in the White House. Moreover, Obama seemed to be saying that Trump used words with no meaning, missing the critical fact that ethno-nationalist authoritarians like Trump craft lies specifically meant to further their particular neofascistic and personal power agendas.

The Detroit speech was Obama's most intense foray against Trump prior to the full-on campaign season of the summer and fall of 2020, which, at the time of this writing, we are descending upon. It is unclear if Obama will break with his custom of treading lightly around his taunting and tyrannical successor. Chances are that he will to some degree, though this will have to be understood within the context of Obama's strong attachment to brutally time-staggered major party elections as the legitimate moment for "democracy" to supposedly find expression.

"A VERY DELIBERATE DECISION"

Two months after the Detroit speech, the *Atlantic*'s Edward-Isaac Dovere pondered Obama's uncertain public politics, reflecting on how "Barack Obama has sometimes struggled to find his political footing since leaving office, *even though he's more popular and more in demand by Democrats than at any point since 2008*. He's been challenged," Dovere wrote, " by a *very deliberate decision he'd made to steer clear of direct confrontation with Donald Trump* for a year and a half, aware that a fight is always exactly what Trump is looking for. Why help him turn out the

Republican base?"[13] [Emphasis added.] This was a very charitable interpretation of Obama's tepidness. Dovere underestimated Obama's deeply conservative nature, reflecting on Obama's "over-generosity" (as Zack Beauchamp put it) towards—and excessive toleration and accommodation of—the right-wing. Why, one might have asked Dovere, should not the highly popular Obama have stoked legitimate popular anger at Trump in order to help turn out the Democratic voting base or, better yet, why shouldn't he have spurred millions in the streets to demand the end of a white nationalist neofascist regime in Washington?

Dovere really showed his excessive Obama sycophancy with a particularly strange claim. In September of 2018, Dovere wrote, Obama "unleashed an intense argument against Trump and carried that forward with considerable effect through the midterms, which produced a blue wave that devastated Republicans nationally and locally." This was sheer nonsense. Obama sparked no such argument and it is far from clear that his few cautious campaign speeches had much if any impact on the mid-term outcomes.

The pattern of Obama avoiding direct confrontation Trump while scoring undeserved points with reporters and liberal commentators for supposedly taking on the president continued after Democrats seized control of the House of Representatives in early 2019. When Trump, in another signature white-nationalist moment, outrageously told four Congresswoman of color to "go back to your crime-infested home countries" in mid-July of 2019, Obama said nothing but scored "fight back" points with some media operatives simply by sharing a Twitter post of a *Washington Post* op-ed. The op-ed condemned Trump's comment and was co-signed by more than 140 African-Americans who had served in the Obama administration. "I've always been proud of what this team accomplished during my administration," Obama wrote above the op-ed. "But more than what we did, I'm proud of how they're continuing to fight for an America that's better." This post was the extent of his response.

"WALKING UP TO THE EDGE OF CONDEMNING TRUMP": AS THOUGH HE WAS STILL PRESIDENT

Two weeks later, a deranged young white racist man who issued a white-nationalist and nativist manifesto consistent with Trump's ideology drove 650 miles to El Paso, Texas, where he massacred twenty-three people with a semi-automatic rifle at a Wal-Mart Supercenter known for its largely Mexican-American customer-base. Another gun massacre conducted by a deranged young white man took place in Dayton, Ohio the very next day. Taken together and seen in the context of the gun violence that continued to plague America, the two terrible incidents illustrated the horrors of the at once racist and gun-saturated white-nationalist culture that Trump had been both tapping and fueling in alliance with the neofascistic National Rifle Association (NRA).

It was a moment that called for an actual "president in exile for [and actual] the political opposition" (to use Van Newkirk II's ironic words) to call out Trump for his nativism, his racism, and his dark alliance with the NRA. Obama did no such thing. Instead, he issued an online statement that, as *The Atlantic*'s David Graham pointed out, "walked up to the edge of condemning Trump, then stopped without naming him":

> No other nation on Earth comes close to experiencing
> the frequency of mass shootings that we see in the United
> States. No other developed nation tolerates the levels of
> gun violence that we do.... All of us have to send a clarion
> call and behave with the values of tolerance and diversity
> that should be the hallmarks of our democracy. We should
> soundly reject language coming out of the mouths of any
> of our leaders that feeds a climate of fear and hatred or
> normalizes racist sentiments; leaders who demonize those
> who don't look like us, or suggest that other people, includ-
> ing immigrants, threaten our way of life, or refer to other

people as sub-human, or imply that America belongs to just one certain type of people…It's time for the overwhelming majority of Americans of goodwill, of every race and faith and political party, to say as much—clearly and unequivocally.

Besides omitting Trump's considerable responsibility for advancing nativism, racism, and gun culture, Obama comments recommended no specific policy suggestions.

Obama, Graham wrote, "continues to act almost as though he is the president. This note reads like a statement released by the Obama White House. Like president Obama, former president Obama wants to remain above the political fray."

This was an important observation. Stuck in the long hangover of his actual presidency, Obama had "never quite figured out how to respond to Trump," Graham felt, because the former president clung to his longstanding arrogant presumption and illusion of being beyond partisan politics and because Obama was overly insistent on trying to "maintain the old norm against former presidents criticizing the current officeholder."

Why on Earth follow that norm during a openly norm-smashing neofascistic presidency that broke numerous presidential norms, including the convention of not obsessively criticizing one's predecessor?[14]

"HE STAYS MUM"

Obama also stayed strangely quiet all during the release of the Mueller Report, Trump's subsequent UkraineGate scandal, and through the President's impeachment in the summer, fall, and early winter of 2019. Apparently he saw no need to comment on vital constitutional and foreign policy issues.

In an important November 2019 *POLITICO* report bearing the revealing title "Waiting for Obama," longtime up-close Obama chronicler Ryan Lizza noted that "once the Democrats took over the House and the enormous Democratic presidential field began to emerge, the demands for him to weigh in on everything receded. These days when his staff brings him ideas, issues, outrages that he might address, Obama always asks a simple question: 'To what end?" More often than not, he stays mum."

DON'T SAY HIS NAME

Even Obama's speech on April 14th, 2020, endorsing Joe Biden as Trump's Democratic opponent, failed to mention Trump by name. Calling for "good government" and respect for "facts and science," Obama opined that "the rule of law matters" and called for "leaders who are informed and honest and who seek to bring people together rather than drive them apart." Obama denounced a "politics that too often has been characterized by corruption, carelessness, self-dealing, disinformation, ignorance and just plain meanness" and vapidly upheld the notion of a "more democratic America where everybody has a fair shot at opportunity." It was a strikingly conservative speech in which Obama could bring himself to mention the Republican Party just once and then just barely: "Democrats may not always agree on every detail of the best way to bring …[positive] change, but we do agree that they are needed and that only happens if we win this election, because one thing everybody has learned by now is that the Republicans occupying the White House and running the U.S. Senate are not interested in progress." Obama evinced no understanding that the Republicans had become the party of Trump, a neofascistic white nationalist trying to (in Chomsky's words) "destroy the prospects for organized human life in Earth in the not-distant future."

COVID QUIETUDE

Not-So "Unvarnished Remarks"

Obama remained essentially mute also as the nation was rocked in the spring and summer of 2020 by the worst pandemic in a century. While the medical science-denying madman Trump plunged the nation deep into epidemiological catastrophe, the forty-fourth president stayed quiet. His silence was deafening. In mid-April, the author and political commentator Drew Magary couldn't take the quietude any longer. He penned a widely read, profanity-laden *Medium* essay titled "Where the Hell is Barack Obama?" Here's some of what Magary wrote:

> Over 20,000 Americans are dead. In a blink, national unemployment levels are about to blow the Great Depression's metrics out of the water. States that are on life support have been forced to compete for vital goods because the federal government has abandoned them. Congress is on fucking VACATION. We're living through a national death spiral. Right now.

> So where are you, Barack Obama? I'm not asking that wistfully. This is not a folk song. I wanna know: WHERE THE FUCK ARE YOU? …The influence that Obama has left on the table has been so staggering as to be obscene. …Obama hasn't so much as lifted a fucking finger to stop President Trump from gleefully dismantling his works, which just so happens to have included a functional national pandemic response infrastructure.

> …Guess what, sleepyhead? THE APOCALYPSE CAME. And where are you? …I'm sick of Barack Obama staying above the fray while that fray is swallowing us whole. It's infuriating…This is Obama frittering away the good will he generated to no discernible good end. It would be nice, for a change, if Barack Obama could emerge from his cave and offer—no wait, DEMAND—a way forward. It would be nice if he went Full Chicago and fucking fought for answers. But he hasn't, and he won't. THIS is what his legacy should be now. Meanwhile, the current president would like virus death to become an accepted and perpetual fact of life here so that his favorite teevee show—AMERICA: IT'S GREAT!—can return from hiatus.

> I'm sorry if I find no solace in any of this. I'm sorry if I don't look at what's going on, with nurses forced to wear fucking trash bags to keep from getting infected, and seeing

it as some grand testament to the American spirit. When you're as well off as Obama, you can afford to have faith in America. Meanwhile, this is the country that elected Donald Trump president. What kind of asshole country does that? Why would ANY sane person have faith in it? If you have faith in America right now, not only is it tone deaf, it's also a luxury no one else can afford. There is no unity. There never was, and there never will be. Take it from AOC: "The whole process of coming together should be uncomfortable for everyone involved—that's how you know it's working. And if (Joe) Biden is only doing things he's comfortable with, then it's not enough….

The longer he refuses to take any public action, the more I'll remember him as a man who said all the right things while, in his cherished long run, not having much to show for it. Wake the fuck up, Mr. President. The arc of the moral universe is no longer long. It is terrifyingly short, and guess which way it's bending?

It is true that in early May of 2020, Obama was quoted by media sources declaring that Trump's response to the COVID-19 crisis had been "an absolute chaotic disaster" and that the "rule of law" was "at risk" because Trump's Justice Department has recently decided to drop charges against former White House national security adviser Michael Flynn, previously convicted for lying to the FBI about his relationship with the Russian government. Obama's comments were leaked from a private phone call with the "Obama Alumni Association," a group of three thousand former staffers from the Obama White House. Yahoo! News reporter and leading RussiaGate author Michael Isikoff wrote that "Obama's *unvarnished remarks were some of his sharpest yet* about the Trump administration and appeared to forecast a dramatically stepped-up political role he intends to play in this year's election" [emphasis added].[15] This was remarkable: by the veteran Washington correspondent Isikoff's estimation, Obama's painfully belated, private, and mild (not-so-"unvarnished") statements of concern about, firstly, a COVID-19 response that had been criminally botched from the very beginning and about, secondly, the latest in a long record of Trump administration assaults on the rule of law were characterized as some of the "sharpest" comments about the Trump administration "yet." And this more than three years into a presidency that had been one long, rolling "chaotic disaster"! Notably, too, Obama's "Alumni Association" comments failed to mention his successor by name.

The same was true of widely-reported comments that Obama made in a May 2020 commencement address that was livestreamed courtesy of the LeBron James Family Foundation to high school graduates and graduates of historically Black colleges and universities. "More than anything, this pandemic has fully, finally torn back the curtain on the idea that so many of the folks in charge know what they're doing," Obama told the graduates, adding that "a lot of them aren't even pretending to be in charge."[16]

Again, Obama understated the magnitude of the disaster in which the nation was mired. His words failed to call out Trump by name, and meanwhile offered tepid criticism of Trump's COVID-19 polices, which were arguably criminal and corrupt, not merely ignorant. Moreover, Obama's milquetoast "rebuke" came long after the extent of Trump's transgressions were first reported.

According to *POLITICO*'s Evan Semones, "The former president, who did not mention President Donald Trump by name, has generally shied away from weighing in on politics or criticizing his successor since leaving office, but has more recently spoken out against the current administration's handling of the coronavirus crisis." This, too, was a an extraordinary observation from a veteran Washington journalist. Even three-plus years into the Trump presidency, Obama could not say Trump's name, and was only now barely breaking away from his practice of "generally sh[ying] away from weighing in on politics or criticizing his successor since leaving office"!

"OBAMA APPEARED TO FIGHT BACK"

His extreme reticence was challenged again in March, when Trump tried to avoid responsibility for his lethal COVID-19 failures by shifting blame for the outbreak on to Obama. The taunts came regularly, with Trump claiming that Obama had undermined the government's capacity to respond. Without any evidence, Trump accused Obama of having imposed onerous regulations that crippled the private sector's ability to generate virus test kits. He even charged that the previous administration had failed to developed accurate tests for the novel coronavirus, either failing to recognize or deliberately "forgetting" that the virus did not exist among humans during the Obama administration.

Finally, at the end of March, the *Washington Post* claimed that "Obama appeared to fight back." So what was Obama's counterpunch? "We've seen all too terribly the consequences of those who denied warnings of a pandemic," he Tweeted. The *Post* followed up by saying that the terse comment "could be read as a critique of Trump's initial efforts to minimize the threat of the pathogen." Obama also linked to a report on the Trump administration's rollback of Obama-era rules to curb auto emissions, adding that "We can't afford any more consequences of climate denial. All of us, especially young people, have to demand better of our government at every level and vote this fall."

That was it. *That* was Obama's "fight back"—a tepid tweet that again failed to mention Trump by name and came with the arch-electoralist's standard reminder that people need to vote.

Obama insiders told the *Post* that the former president's "political…message was aimed at holding a broad group of Republican politicians accountable for dismissing climate science" and that Obama had made a "decision to step into the political arena amid the lethal spread of the novel coronavirus." This revelation seemed to suggest that Trump was just one among a large collection of GOP politicos, not a lethal agent of ecocide in the world's most powerful office at a moment of grave environmental peril. Why the *Post* believed that indirect tweets were much of a "step into the political arena" was unclear.

And where had Obama been in 2018 when Trump dismantled a White House National Security Council directorate whose mission was to prepare for a major pandemic that virtually every expert believed would inevitably hit the United States? It was a consequential rollback. As the Associated Press reported last March 14th:

> Public health and national security experts [have] been warning about the next pandemic for years and criticized the Trump administration's decision in 2018 to dismantle a National Security Council directorate at the White House charged with preparing for when, not if, another pandemic would hit the nation.
>
> "It would be nice if the office was still there," Dr. Anthony Fauci, the director of the National Institute of Allergy and Infectious Diseases at the National Institute of Health, told Congress this week. "I wouldn't necessarily characterize it as a mistake (to eliminate the unit). I would say we worked very well with that office."
>
> The NSC directorate for global health and security and bio-defense survived the transition from President Barack Obama to Trump in 2017.
>
> Trump's elimination of the office suggested, along with his proposed budget cuts for the CDC, that he did not see the threat of pandemics in the same way that many experts in the field did.
>
> "One year later I was mystified when the White House dissolved the office, leaving the country less prepared for pandemics like COVID-19," Beth Cameron, the first director of the unit, wrote in an op-ed Friday in the *Washington Post*.
>
> She said the directorate was set up to be the "smoke alarm" and get ahead of emergencies and sound a warning at the earliest sign of fire—"all with the goal of avoiding a six-alarm fire."

It's impossible to assess the impact of the 2018 decision to disband the unit, she said. Cameron noted that biological experts remain at the White House, but she says it's clear that eliminating the office contributed to what she called a "sluggish domestic response." She said that shortly before Trump took office, the unit was watching a rising number of cases in China of a deadly strain of the flu and a yellow fever outbreak in Angola.

Obama said nothing about the pandemic office's closing at the time. He rang no alarms.

"A TRICKY BALANCE"

"I think there's a tricky balance here," said Jen Psaki, a former communications director from the Obama White House when asked by reporters about Obama's weak response to Trump's absurd coronavirus hecklings. "As much as former president Obama has an enormous microphone and people still look to hear what he has to say" Psaki explained, "he also, especially at a time of global crisis, *does not want to create a moment that's perceived as political*—a battle between a former Democratic president and a sitting Republican president, even if President Trump is completely mishandling this."[17] As if public health policy weren't a political matter.

NOT-SO "MOUNTED PUBLIC DEFENSES" OF OBAMA'S OWN SIGNATURE POLICIES

"A Right for Everybody"

A "tricky balance"? So what if hundreds of thousands of Obama's fellow Americans were slated to die because of Trump's egregious and criminal failures? A sampling of Obama's associates told the *Washington Post* that Obama's tweet was "consistent with his pledge to speak out judiciously when Trump's efforts to roll back his signature policies threaten to undermine the public good. Obama," the *Post* reported, "has *mounted public defenses* against the Trump administration's bid to unwind the Affordable Care Act (ACA), the Paris climate accord, the Iran nuclear deal and a deferred action program (DACA) for younger undocumented immigrants."

Really? Of what did these "mounted public defenses" consist? Regarding the ACA, Obama responded to Trump-Republican efforts to undo it by issuing a statement on the legislation's seventh anniversary in March 2017. Obama's proclamation hailed the bill for expanding coverage to twenty million Americans, including people formerly denied coverage thanks to pre-existing conditions. In his standard corporate, neoliberal language, Obama claimed that the ACA had slowed the pace of health care system inflation, boosted job growth, and "stabilized" health care markets. Obama claimed, too, that "We finally declared that in America, health care is not a privilege for a few, but a right for everybody," ignoring the fact that Obamacare left several million Americans without insurance or affordable care, and kept the nation saddled with an absurdly expensive, poorly performing, and savagely unequal health care stystem largely because of the program's commitment to private health insurance, drug companies, and the broad for-profit medical industrial complex. The former president's final paragraph was fake-progressive mendacity at its best:

> The Affordable Care Act is law only because millions of Americans mobilized, and organized, and decided that this fight was about more than health care—it was about the character of our country. It was about whether the wealthiest nation on Earth would make sure that neither illness nor twist of fate would rob us of everything we've worked so hard to build. It was about whether we look out for one another, as neighbors, and fellow citizens, who care about each other's success.[18]

Obama's false boasts were unaccompanied by any reference to how Trump and the Republicans were trying to kick twenty million Americans off of health insurance in the name of liberating the nation from supposedly "socialist" Obamacare.

"THE PRIVATE SECTOR ALREADY CHOSE A LOW-CARBON FUTURE"

In June of 2017, Trump announced his decision to withdraw the United States from the supposed "job-killing" 2015 Paris Climate Agreement. The move was in accordance with his "America First" policy. Trump accompanied his attack on this signature Obama administration achievement with the absurd claim that the Paris Accord "undermine[s] (the U.S.) economy" and "puts [the U.S.] at a permanent disadvantage." Obama responded with a bland, sanctimonious, and classically neoliberal official statement badly minimizing Trump's action. The forty-fourth president made no reference to the grave dangers posed by the climate crisis or Trump's threats to a livable planet. Instead, Obama oversold the accord, which fell far short of the sort of enforceable benchmarks required to stem catastrophic climate change. He falsely thrust the United States into the global climate protection vanguard and incorrectly claimed that private capital was already putting the world on a path to a low-carbon future anyway:

> A year and a half ago, the world came together in Paris around the first-ever global agreement to set the world on a low-carbon course and protect the world we leave to our children.
>
> It was steady, principled American leadership on the world stage that made that achievement possible. It was bold American ambition that encouraged dozens of other nations to set their sights higher as well. And what made that leadership and ambition possible was America's private innovation and public investment in growing industries like wind and solar—industries that created some of the fastest new streams of good-paying jobs in recent years, and contributed to the longest streak of job creation in our history.

Simply put, the private sector already chose a low-carbon future. And for the nations that committed themselves to that future, the Paris Agreement opened the floodgates for businesses, scientists, and engineers to unleash high-tech, low-carbon investment and innovation on an unprecedented scale.

The nations that remain in the Paris Agreement will be the nations that reap the benefits in jobs and industries created. I believe the United States of America should be at the front of the pack. But even in the absence of American leadership; even as this Administration joins a small handful of nations that reject the future; I'm confident that our states, cities, and businesses will step up and do even more to lead the way, and help protect for future generations the one planet we've got.[19]

"WE ALL KNOW THE DANGERS OF IRAN"

Consistent with candidate Trump's repeated claims that "Obama's nuclear deal with Iran" was a "total disaster," the Trump administration announced it would withdraw from another of Obama's "signature" 2015 policies—the Joint Comprehensive Plan of Action (JCPOA), also known as the "Iran nuclear deal," in early May of 2018. The JCPOA is an agreement on Iran's nuclear program reached in July 2015 by Iran and the P5+1 (the five permanent members of the United Nations Security Council— China, France, Russia, United Kingdom, United States—plus Germany). Under the agreement's terms, Iran consented to restrictions that would allow it to have enough enriched uranium to meet its domestic energy needs without possessing the capacity to build a nuclear bomb. Iran also agreed to allow inspectors from the United Nations' International Atomic Energy Agency (IAEA) to monitor its energy and weapons facilities. When Trump announced U.S. withdrawal from the agreement, he falsely claimed that Obama was letting Iran develop nuclear weapons capabilities. In fact, the IAEA had repeatedly found

Iran to be complying with the terms of the pact, undermining Trump's claim.

Obama's response to Trump's actions, which also re-imposed crippling economic sanctions on Iran, was another sanctimonious and elegantly worded official statement that failed to mention Trump by name. Obama said nothing about the racism lurking behind Trump's action and repeated the longstanding U.S.-imperialist lie—shared with Trump and with the aggressive murderous U.S. client states Israel and Saudi Arabia—that Iran is a malevolent and dangerous actor posing a serious threat of nuclear war in the Middle East:

> There are few issues more important to the security of the United States than the potential spread of nuclear weapons, or the potential for even more destructive war in the Middle East. That's why the United States negotiated the Joint Comprehensive Plan of Action (JCPOA) in the first place.
>
> The reality is clear. The JCPOA is working—that is a view shared by our European allies, independent experts, and the current U.S. Secretary of Defense. The JCPOA is in America's interest—it has significantly rolled back Iran's nuclear program….That is why today's announcement is so misguided. Walking away from the JCPOA turns our back on America's closest allies, and an agreement that our country's leading diplomats, scientists, and intelligence professionals negotiated. In a democracy, there will always be changes in policies and priorities from one Administration to the next. But the consistent flouting of agreements that our country is a party to risks eroding America's credibility, and puts us at odds with the world's major powers… Without the JCPOA, the United States could eventually be left with a losing choice between a nuclear-armed Iran or another war in the Middle East. We all know the dangers of Iran obtaining a nuclear weapon. It could embolden an already dangerous regime; threaten our friends with destruction; pose unacceptable dangers to America's own security; and trigger an arms race in the world's most dangerous region. If the constraints on Iran's nuclear program under the JCPOA are lost, we could be hastening the day

when we are faced with the choice between living with that threat, or going to war to prevent it.

In a dangerous world, America must be able to rely in part on strong, principled diplomacy to secure our country. We have been safer in the years since we achieved the JCPOA, thanks in part to the work of our diplomats, many members of Congress, and our allies. Going forward, I hope that Americans continue to speak out in support of the kind of strong, principled, fact-based, and unifying leadership that can best secure our country and uphold our responsibilities around the globe.

As Obama certainly knew but would never have admitted in public, Iran was and is no great regional threat. The real enemies of peace, stability, democracy, and human decency in the Middle East have long been and remain the U.S.-allied regional powers—the harshly repressive absolutist Saudi regime (possibly the most reactionary government on Earth) and the apartheid and occupation state of Israel.

"THIS IS ABOUT BASIC DECENCY"

What about DACA, Obama's 2012 executive order shielding from deportation 700,000 young, undocumented, and "law-abiding" immigrant adults who were brought to the U.S. as children, allowing them to work, attend school, and receive public benefits in the U.S.? When Trump ordered the end of DACA in September of 2017, Obama responded with a carefully crafted statement that failed (once again) to mention Trump by name or to address the viciously racist nativism behind the action. In standard Obama style, the former president sanctimoniously appealed to Americans to be good and virtuous and proclaimed his faith in the nation's reigning institutions to make things right:

It is precisely because this action is contrary to our spirit, and to common sense, that business leaders, faith leaders, economists, and Americans of all political stripes called on

the administration not to do what it did today. And now
that the White House has shifted its responsibility for these
young people to Congress, it's up to Members of Congress
to protect these young people and our future. I'm heartened
by those who've suggested that they should. And I join my
voice with the majority of Americans who hope they step
up and do it with a sense of moral urgency that matches the
urgency these young people feel.

Ultimately, this is about basic decency. This is about
whether we are a people who kick hopeful young strivers
out of America, or whether we treat them the way we'd
want our own kids to be treated. It's about who we are as a
people—and who we want to be.

What makes us American is not a question of what we
look like, or where our names come from, or the way we
pray. What makes us American is our fidelity to a set of
ideals—that all of us are created equal; that all of us deserve
the chance to make of our lives what we will; that all of us
share an obligation to stand up, speak out, and secure our
most cherished values for the next generation. That's how
America has traveled this far. That's how, if we keep at it, we
will ultimately reach that more perfect union.

Obama naturally had nothing to say about how much of "the
union" called the United States was stolen from the nation in
which most of the DACA "recipients" were born—Mexico.

SAY HIS NAME

If ever there was a time for the nation's first Black president to
have stepped up and called out Trump for his racism and fascism,
the weeks of protest that followed the murder of George Floyd in
Minneapolis was the time. Sadly, however, Obama had nothing
to say about Trump's shockingly "fascist performance" (Masha
Gessen) during the remarkable multi-racial demonstrations that
erupted in late May of 2020, demonstrations which continued
into the summer. Instead, on June 3rd, Obama responded with a
livestream talk that (again) never mentioned Trump's name and

said nothing about Trump's chilling, neofascistic, racist response to the demonstrations. Nor did he question the institutions that were targeted by the protesters. Obama praised "the folks in law enforcement who share the goals of re-imagining police." He furthered claimed that good police were "just as outraged by the tragedies of recent weeks as are many of the protesters. We're grateful for the vast majority of you who protect and serve... because you're a part of the solution."

What did Obama recommend? He trumpeted his own administration's squishy blue-ribbon "Task Force on 21st Century Policing," which "included law enforcement" in developing "a very specific set of recommendations" to "strengthen public trust and foster better working relationships between law enforcement and communities that they're supposed to protect even as they're continuing to promote effective reduction." "Change" would happen at the local level, Obama said, counseling protesters to "find practical" and "evidence-based solutions" and focus on the election of smart and empathetic mayors, city councilpersons, prosecutors, sheriffs, judges, and police review boards. Obama's basic point was that activists should cool their jets and work within the system to elect corporate, professional class technocrats like himself who speak in the language of the professional class, and who serve and protect, furthermore, the corporate elite and its assets. For good measure, Obama called for Americans to give money to the Obama Foundation's My Brothers' Keeper (MBK) initiative. MBK is a conservative, Urban League-style program wherein the corporate-funded Black bourgeoisie tries to make poor Black men respectable and properly suited to white capitalist society.

Obama had nothing to say, moreover, about the Trumpian police state outrages that were occurring across the country, including the killing of a young female protestor in Columbus, Ohio and the incidents such as those detailed below, originally related to me by one of my history students in Chicago, Obama's supposed "home town":

> As the crowd worked their way up to Trump Tower, there were chants and signs referring to George Floyd and the Black Lives Matter movement....Once the protestors made it to the Trump Tower, there was a moment of silence for George Floyd and the other black lives lost due to police brutality. This was when the protest started to get more assertive, and officers started to mace, tear gas and shoot rubber bullets at the protestors. Three different people were shot in the head with rubber bullets and needed immediate medical care to stop excessive bleeding or to save an eye. At this time, the protestors started to fight back to stop arrests from happening....This was when I realized that it was starting to get very intense and the cops were trying to strategically lock all the protestors in by closing down public transportation and lifting all the bridges. I decided to leave with my group and made it home safely before I was stuck in a bad situation. This peaceful protest turned into pure chaos, thanks to the police. The city was put on curfew lockdown allowing cops to arrest anyone who was out past 9, which in itself is another problem by allowing the police to pick and choose who they want to arrest based on this curfew.

Along the way, Obama used the Movement for Black Lives as an opportunity to take another one of his many ongoing, elitist shots at the 1960s:

> I've heard some people say that you have a pandemic, then you have these protests, this reminds people of the '60s and the chaos and the discord and distrust throughout the country. I have to tell you, although I was very young ... I know enough about that history to say there is something different....You look at the protests and that was a far more representative cross-section of America out on the streets peacefully protesting who felt moved to do something because the instance they had seen injustice. That didn't exist in the 1960s, that kind of broad coalition.

Here again, as he did when he first emerged as a presidential contender in 2006, Obama slandered the great popular movements of the 1960s. As participants recall and scholars have demonstrated, those movements involved broad coalitions with vast "cross sections of America out on the streets peacefully protesting because they had seen injustice," Obama's claims notwithstanding.

"OUT OF RETIREMENT," SORT OF

A long *New York Times* feature that appeared late in June 2020 bore an enticing title: "The Trump Campaign is Drawing Obama Out of Retirement." As evidence for their thesis that Obama was forsaking his prior post-presidential "retirement vision—a placid life that was to consist of writing, sun-flecked fairways, policy work through his foundation, producing documentaries with Netflix and family time aplenty at a new $11.7 million spread on Martha's Vineyard" to enter the fray against his apocalyptic successor, *Times* reporters Glenn Thrush and Elaina Plott noted that Obama closely monitored the polling numbers of Trump and presumptive Democratic presidential candidate Joe Biden, and "takes pride in the fact that he has millions more Twitter followers than a president who relies on the platform far more than he does." Thrush and Plott added that Obama "devours online news" late into the night, sending off "round[s] of texts, often about the latest Trump outrage" to friends and contacting his first attorney general Eric Holder to complain about Trump Attorney General William Barr's role in the violent repression of protesters outside the White House during the Movement for Black Lives protests. Above all, the *Times* reporters were impressed that Obama had recently "stepped up his nominally indirect criticism of Mr. Trump's administration" by complaining about a "shambolic, disorganized, meanspirited approach to governance" during an online Biden fundraiser.

Thrush and Plott mused that Obama's "instinct to refrain from a brawl that he fear may dent his popularity and challenge his place in history" was "changing in the wake of George Floyd's killing" and the social justice uprising the murder helped spawn. In reality, the signs of Obama's supposed rise from the shadows reported by the *Times* were rather weak. The supposedly newly aroused Obama that Thrush and Plott portrayed on the basis of interviews with Obama's friends and associates remained absurdly reluctant to call out Trump and Trumpism by name. He limited most of his "anti-Trump" commentary to private communications with current and former associates. Furthermore, Thrush and Plott learned that Obama absurdly refused to call Trump a racist "even in private, preferring a more indirect accusation of 'racial demagoguery.'"

But Thrush and Plott missed a key point by not following up on the issue of Obama's pride in his Twitter following. Curiously enough, given the fact that Obama was proudly conscious that more people read his Tweets than Trump's Tweets, the former president's use of Twitter dwindled precipitously after he left the White House, sinking to a frequency of less than one a day. It was another example of Obama deigning to use a key weapon in his hands. "Obama," Lizza observed in his aforementioned November 2019 report, "has the most followed Twitter account in the world, but rather than use it as a political weapon, he acts more like a celebrity social media influencer." The online Obama "tried to maintain a sense of normalcy," Lizza found: "His social media became an unusual mix of book and movie recommendations, appeals to help the victims of natural disasters, and tributes to statesmen or celebrities who passed."

THIS GUY

As this book approached publication in late July, the Joe Biden campaign released a campaign video featuring a 15-minute, socially distanced conversation between Biden and his former boss Obama at the former president's headquarters in Washington D.C. Neither Biden nor Obama mentioned Trump's name once as they expressed carefully worded disdain for "this guy's" (Trump's) failure and indeed open refusal to take responsibility for the COVID-19 crisis. Biden and Trump were also properly revolted by "this guy's" attempt to throw millions of Americans off of health insurance in the middle of a pandemic. The conversation included numerous deceptive boasts about the Obama administration's supposed desire to have included a health insurance "public option" in Obamacare (a truly disingenuous claim). Obama tried to tap the suburban electorate's concerns about the anti-science sociopath Trump by identifying Biden with the values of "empathy" and "pay[ing] attention to science." "It all starts with being able to relate. If you can sit down with a family and see your own family in them....then you're going to work hard for them. And that's what's always what's motivated you to get into public service." Obama also praised Biden for a "willingness to listen and learn."

"Much of the video," the liberal *Huffington Post* reported, "contrast[ed] President Donald Trump's failure to contain the COVID-19 crisis with what Biden would do instead, as well as other areas where Trump has failed to demonstrate any leadership or empathy." The report was accurate but left out the remarkable extent to which Obama and the Biden team went to avoid any direct reference either to Trump by name or to the virulent white-nationalist neo-fascism he represented. It was almost surreal to watch the tepid video on July 24th as Trump threatened to send out 75,000 federal agents to repress urban Americans—this as federal unemployment benefits ran out and a federal ban on evictions expired amidst the onset of a second Great Depression.

THE JOHN LEWIS FUNERAL ORATION

The highwater mark of Obama's willingness to speak out force-fully against Trump before this book went to press (on August 2, 2020) came from a chance event: the death of the onetime Black Civil Rights icon and longtime U.S. Representative John Lewis (D-GA) at the end of July. In a polished forty-minute oration eulogizing Lewis before a mostly Black audience, Obama spoke passionately against how "those in power...are doing their darnedest to discourage people from voting by closing polling locations, and targeting minorities and students with restrictive ID laws, and attacking our voting rights with surgical precision—even undermining the Postal Service in the run-up to an election that's going to be dependent on mail-in ballots so people don't get sick." Obama also spoke with anger and eloquence against how "we can witness our federal government sending agents to use tear gas and batons against peaceful demonstrators."

But Obama still could not bring himself to mention Trump by name or to use the F-word—fascism—that he had rightly applied to Trump in his private conversation with Tim Kaine in October of 2016. Obama failed to mention the Trump paramilitaries' use of deadly rubber bullets and other "impact munitions," and he said nothing about the remarkable popular anti-fascist upris-ing that forced a paramilitary retreat in Portland. Obama badly devalued the significance of social movement protest beyond the election cycle—the very type of political engagement that had brought John Lewis on to the stage of history—by telling his audience that "the right to vote" is "the most powerful tool we have" and that voting is "the most important action we can take on behalf of democracy." His speech ended with vapid references to the gradual and supposed forward march of American history toward "a more perfect union."

The New York Times reported that "Mr. Obama lacerated his successor, though not by name." Lest mentioning Obama's amazingly persistent failure to name Trump might make the former president sound too tame, *Times* reporters Maggie Astor and Shane Goldmacher added that "in recent private chats with Democratic donors, Mr. Obama has hit Mr. Trump more directly, accusing him of campaigning by stirring up 'nativist, racist, sexist' resentments…" Astor and Goldmacher had nothing to say about the apparently continuing and telling difference between the more candid, direct, and forceful things Obama says about Trump *to wealthy elites in private* and *the milder and more indirect things* he says about the unnamed forty-fifth president *in public*.

A FINAL IRONY

To be a Left critic of the Obama presidency (as was the present author) was to face the recurrent and absurd charge from Democrats that one was a racially suspect (racist) Republican and Tea Partier. It did not seem to matter that Obama's portside faultfinders had commonly outdone their accusers when it came to criticism of and resistance to the right-wing George W. Bush presidency. The charge came anyway from liberal and moderate Democrats who were unwilling and/or unable to process the existence of sharp political minds standing to the left of both of the nation's reigning corporate parties. Now, we are living under the most vicious right-wing presidency in modern U.S. history, and it is worthwhile to note a curious irony: most of Obama's left critics are far more regularly and harshly critical of the racist, obsessively Obama-denigrating Trump administration than Obama is himself. The man Trump goes out of his way to torment, trash, taunt, and extinguish from history has had incredibly little, all things considered, to say about a president he knew all too well to be a "fascist" before handing the keys of presidential power to the current chief executive.

ENDNOTES

1.   The Leadership Conference on Civil and Human Rights, "Trump Administration Civil and Human Rights Rollbacks," 2020, https://civilrights.

org/trump-rollbacks/?fbclid=IwAR2S8oZStqGYmyUR0MdsrJZdez1e-JpyYj9AW0QrzcyfoStfiJq78F-qHO1M

2   Ben Parker, Stephanie Steinbrecher, Kelsey Ronan, John McMurtrie, Sophia Durose, Rachel Villa, Amy Sumerton, "Lest We Forget the Horrors: A Catalog of Trump's Worst Cruelties, Collusions, Corruptions, and Crimes," *McSweeney's*, 2020, https://www.mcsweeneys.net/articles/the-complete-listing-so-far-atrocities-1-759?Fbclid=iwar2z8byzadk1rstiwbswkvqy5jvlqsb-jcmu1g188go1m3muxc-fay7-3xsq

3. Brent Griffiths, "Obama: I Will Speak Up When Our Core Values Are at Stake," *POLITICO,* January 18, 2017, https://www.politico.com/story/2017/01/obama-last-press-conference-core-values-233780

4. Glenn Thrush and Elaina Plott, "How the Trump Campaign is Drawing Obama Out of Retirement," *New York Times*, June 28, 2020

5. Jessica Taylor, "Obama Criticizes Trump's Travel Ban, Says 'Values Are At Stake,'" NPR January 30, 2017 https://www.npr.org/2017/01/30/512487565/obama-criticizes-trumps-immigration-ban-heartened-by-protests

6. Julian Zelizer, "Obama's Stern Warning for Trump," *CNN,* January 16, 2018, https://www.cnn.com/2018/01/13/opinions/trump-comment-and-our-tolerance-zelizer-opinion/index.html

7. Max Greenwood, "Obama on Trump: How Card Can It Be to Say 'Nazis Are Bad'?," *The Hill,* September 7, 2018, https://thehill.com/homenews/news/405576-obama-how-hard-can-it-be-to-say-nazis-are-bad

8. *POLITICO* Staff, "Transcript: Former President Obama's Speech at the University of Illinois," *POLITICO,* September 7, 2018, https://www.politico.com/story/2018/09/07/obama-university-of-illinois-speech-811130

9. Ibid.

10. Zack Beauchamp, "Barack Obama Just Reminded Us What We've Lost," *Vox,* July 9, 2018, https://www.vox.com/policy-and-politics/2018/7/19/17585896/barack-obama-speech-south-africa-mandela

11. Vann R. Newkirk II, "Obama Still Doesn't Understand Trump," *The Atlantic,* July 20, 2018, https://www.theatlantic.com/politics/archive/2018/07/barack-obama-donald-trump-nationalism/565724/

12. https://www.washingtonpost.com/politics/2020/06/01/president-trump-made-19127-false-or-misleading-claims-1226-days/

13. Edward-Isaac Dovere, "Barack Obama Goes All In Politically to Fight Gerrymandering," *The Atlantic,* December 20, 2018, https://www.theatlantic.com/politics/archive/2018/12/obamas-political-group-shifts-focus-gerrymandering/578770/

14. David A. Graham, "Obama Still Sounds Like a president," The *Atlantic*, August 5, 2019.

15. Michael Isakoff, "Exclusive: Obama Says in Private Call That 'Rule of Law is at Risk'in Michael Flynn Case," *Yahoo! News,* May 8, 2020, https://sports.yahoo.com/obama-irule-of-law-michael-flynn-case-014121045.html

16. https://www.washingtonpost.com/nation/2020/05/16/obama-commencement-speech-2020/

17. David Nakamura, "'A tricky balance': Obama seeks to inform and reassure the public on coronavirus while avoiding confrontation with Trump," the *Washington Post*, March 31, 2020, washingtonpost.com/politics/a-tricky-balance-obama-seeks-to-inform-and-reassure-the-public-on-coronavirus-while-avoiding-confrontation-with-trump/2020/03/31/e1f12b7a-7368-11ea-87da-77a8136c1a6d_story.html

18. Bob Bryan, "Obama Defends ObamaCare: 'America Is Stronger Because of the Affordable Care Act," *Business Insider,* March 23, 2017, https://www.businessinsider.com/barack-obama-statement-on-obamacare-affordable-care-act-2017-3

19. Jean-Michel Cousteau's Ocean Futures Society, "Barack Obama Responds to Withdrawal from Climate Paris Deal," http://oceanfutures.org/barack-obama-responds-to-withdrawal-from-paris-climate-deal

CHAPTER 3
Barack Von Obombdenburg

> What matters is not so much the color of your skin as the
> power you serve and the millions you betray.
> —Frantz Fanon, 1952

> Ever since Plato and Aristotle wrote on the topic, political
> theorists have known that democracy cannot flourish on
> soil poisoned by inequality…the resentments bred by such
> divisions are tempting targets for demagogues…
> —Jason Stanley, 2017

> Don't piss down my back and tell me it's raining.
> —An old working-class slogan

There's an old working-class maxim worth keeping in mind when contemplating two of Barack Obama's most stealthily audacious comments during Trump's first year in office: "Don't piss down my back and tell it's raining."

YOU HAVE TO TEND TO THIS GARDEN OF DEMOCRACY

Fewer than five months after handing off the "baton" of freedom to a semi-human oligarch (a "feral wild animal" in the words of one of Trump's most distinguished biographers[1]) who he privately knew to be a "fascist," and who he couldn't bring himself to forthrightly oppose in public, Obama received a "Profiles in Courage" award from the John F. Kennedy Library Foundation in Boston.

"We live," Obama said in his acceptance speech at the Kennedy Library, "in a time of great cynicism about our institutions…It's a cynicism that's most corrosive when it comes to our system of self-government, that clouds our history of jagged, sometimes tentative but ultimately forward progress, that impedes our children's ability to see in the noisy and often too trivial pursuits of politics the possibility of our democracy doing big things."

Nobody in the tuxedo- and evening gown-wearing crowd stood up to tell "Wall Street Barry" that the U.S. had no "system of self-government," no real functioning democracy" to speak of. Nobody rose to observe that, as the mainstream political scientists Martine Gilens and Benjamin Page had shown six years into Obama's presidency, the nation had for decades been "an oligarchy" where wealthy "elites" and their corporations "rule" and "ordinary citizens have virtually no influence over what their government does."

Obama inveighed against those in elected office who showed cowardice by serving the wealthy few instead of the common good. "It actually doesn't take a lot of courage," Obama observed, "to aid those who are already powerful, already comfortable, already influential."

Seven months later, Obama gave his first major public address since Trump's election at the posh and corporate Economic Club of Chicago—a fitting setting, given how his political rise had depended on his connections with Chicago's wealthy and powerful elite.

"You have," Obama told his well-heeled business class audience during a Q&A after the talk, "to tend to this garden of democracy. Otherwise," Obama warned, "*things can fall apart fairly quickly.*"

By "fall apart fairly quickly," Obama meant, perhaps, that the country could descend into authoritarianism and even, though he did not use the word, fascism. The former president made a somewhat awkward and indirect but unmistakable reference to the rise of Adolph Hitler's Third Reich. "We've seen societies where that happens," Obama said, adding this: "Now, presumably there was a ballroom here in Vienna in the late 1920s or '30s that looked pretty sophisticated and seemed as if it, filled with the music and art and literature that was emerging, would continue into perpetuity. And then 60 million people died. An entire world was plunged into chaos…So you got to pay attention—and vote!"[2]

It was quite an historical reference, rendered more ominous by Obama saying "here in Vienna." In his first major public appearance since Trump's election, Obama made an analogy to Weimar Germany, which gave way to fascism when Germany's President Paul Von Hindenburg appointed Adolph Hitler, the leader of the Nazi Party, Chancellor in January of 1933. Von Hindenburg would honor Hitler's "advice" by issuing the "Reichstag Fire Decree" on February 28, 1933. The decree nullified key German civil liberties, providing the "legal basis" for the imprisonment of non- and anti-Nazis, the suppression of publications considered unfriendly to the fascist cause, and the broad establishment of a one-party Nazi state in Germany.

A BLUNT NEO-WEIMARIAN LESSON ABOUT POWER

It is difficult for anyone familiar with the actual record of the militantly corporatist and Wall Street-friendly Obama administration to read these comments without a sense of Obama's truly audacious and Orwellian chutzpah.

Did Obama seriously think that nobody in his Kennedy Library audience knew that his administration had engaged in precisely the conduct he was now criticizing by acting "to aid those who are already powerful, already comfortable, already influential"?

"Tend to" the "garden" of American "democracy"? Is that what Obama expected his listeners in Chicago to think he did while in the White House? Seriously?

Beneath expertly crafted fake-progressive imagery and branding, Obama rose to power in Washington with remarkable, record-setting financial backing from Wall Street and K Street election investors. As Obama knew, cultivating the gardens of popular self-rule was not the mission behind their investment. "It's not always clear what Obama's financial backers want," the progressive journalist Ken Silverstein noted in a *Harpers'* report titled "Obama, Inc." in the Fall of 2006, "but it seems safe to conclude that his campaign contributors are not interested merely in clean government and political reform...On condition of anonymity," Silverstein added, "one Washington lobbyist I spoke with was willing to point out the obvious: that big donors would not be helping out Obama if they didn't see him as a 'player.' The lobbyist added: 'What's the dollar value of a starry-eyed idealist?'"

An answer to the lobbyist's question came less the three years later: priceless. In his book *Confidence Men: Wall Street, Washington, and the Education of a President* (2011), the Pulitzer Prize-winning author Ron Suskind told a remarkable story from March of 2009. Three months into Obama's presidency, popular rage at Wall Street was intense. The leading financial institutions were vulnerable and on the defensive. The nation's financial elite had driven the nation and world's economy into an epic meltdown in the period since Silverstein's essay was published, and millions knew it. Having ridden into office partly on a wave of popular anger at the economic power elite's staggering malfeasance, Obama called a meeting of the nation's top thirteen financial executives at the White House. The banking titans came into the meeting full of dread, expecting that the new president would be angry at their monumental negligence and criminality, ready to initiate massive financial reform. Instead, they were pleased to learn that the new president was in their camp. Rather than stand up for those who had been harmed most by the crisis— workers, minorities, and the poor—Obama sided unequivocally with those who had caused the meltdown.

"My administration is the only thing between you and the pitchforks," Obama told the financial oligarchs. "You guys have an acute public relations problem that's turning into a political problem. And I want to help...*I'm not here to go after you. I'm protecting you...I'm going to shield you from congressional and public anger.*" [Emphasis added.]

For the banking elite, who had destroyed millions of jobs and created junk mortgages that cost millions more their homes, there was, as Suskind puts it, "Nothing to worry about. Whereas [President Franklin Delano] Roosevelt had [during the Great Depression] pushed for tough, viciously opposed reforms of Wall Street and famously said 'I welcome their hate,' Obama was saying 'How can I help?'" As one leading banker told Suskind, "The sense of everyone after the meeting was relief. The president had us at a moment of real vulnerability. At that point, he could have ordered us to do just about anything and we would have rolled over. But he didn't—he mostly wanted to help us out, to quell the mob."

The massive taxpayer-funded bailout of the elite banking sector would be only the first chapter in an ongoing story of super fat-cats directing the Obama administration's actions. In coming years, Obama would show his worth to those at the top by doling out numerous forms of corporate welfare to the parasitic rich and powerful. This largesse was unaccompanied by any serious effort to regulate the bankers' conduct or by any remotely comparable bailout for the millions evicted from homes and left unemployed by the not-so invisible hand of the marketplace. No wonder ninety-five percent of national U.S. income gains went to the top 1% during Obama's first term.

It was a critical moment. With Democratic majorities in both houses of Congress and an angry, "pitchfork"-wielding populace at the gates, an actually progressive President Obama could have rallied the populace to push back against the nation's concentrated wealth and power structures by moving ahead aggressively with a number of policies: a stimulus with major public works jobs programs; real (single-payer) health insurance reform; the serious disciplining and even break-up or nationalization of the leading financial institutions; massive federal housing assistance and mortgage relief; and passage of the Employee Free Choice Act, which would have re-legalized union organizing in the U.S. But no such policy initiatives issued from the White House, which opted instead to give the U.S. populace what William Greider memorably called "a blunt lesson about power, who has it and who doesn't." Americans, Greider wrote, "watched Washington rush to rescue the very financial interests that caused the catastrophe. They learned that government has plenty of money to spend when the right people want it. 'Where's my bailout,' became the rueful punch line at lunch counters and construction sites nationwide. Then to deepen the insult, people watched as establishment forces re-launched their campaign for 'entitlement reform'—a euphemism for whacking Social Security benefits, Medicare and Medicaid."

Americans also watched as Obama moved on to pass a health insurance reform (the so-called Affordable Care Act) that only the big insurance and drug companies could love, kicking the popular alternative (single-payer "Medicare for All") to the curb. Originally drafted by the deeply conservative Heritage Foundation and first carried out in Massachusetts by the arch-One Percenter Mitt Romney, the ACA was passed in Congress thanks to Obama's leverage. And then "Wall Street Barry" further demonstrated his "dollar value" by offering the Republicans bigger cuts in Social Security and Medicare than they asked for, as part of his "Grand Bargain" extended during the elite-manufactured debt-ceiling crisis. It was at this point that hundreds of thousands of mostly young Americans demonstrated that they had had enough of Obama's "blunt lesson about power." They formed the Occupy Wall Street Movement, which sought progressive change through direct action and social movement-building rather than through corporate-captive electoral politics.

We will never know how far Occupy might have gone. It was shut down by a federally coordinated campaign of repression that was jointly administered by the Obama administration and hundreds of mostly Democratic city governments—even as the Democrats selectively appropriated Occupy's rhetoric for use against the plutocratic Mitt Romney and his fellow Republicans in 2012.

Obama closed out his presidency by steadily but unsuccessfully working to pass the corporate-globalist Trans-Pacific Partnership, a classically neoliberal and so-called free trade agreement that had been under secret construction by multinational corporate lawyers and corporatist government officials for at least a decade.

How was that for some "progressive neoliberalism?" How Weimar-Germanic and democracy-canceling was that?

WOLIN'S PROPHECY

In his 2008 book *Democracy Incorporated: Corporate-Managed Democracy and the Specter of Inverted Totalitarianism,* published just half a year before Obama was elected, the Princeton philosopher Sheldon Wolin laid out what was to come. "Should Democrats somehow be elected," Wolin prophesied, they would do nothing to "alter significantly the direction of society" or "substantially revers[e] the drift rightwards…The timidity of a Democratic Party mesmerized by centrist precepts," Wolin wrote, "points to the crucial fact that for the poor, minorities, the working class and anti-corporatists there is no opposition party working on their behalf." The corporatist Democrats would work to "marginalize any possible threat to the corporate allies of the Republicans."

These were prescient words. Later that year, a nominal Democrat was elected president, and Democrats comprised the majorities of both houses of Congress. What followed under Obama (as under his Democratic presidential predecessor Bill Clinton) was the standard "elite" corporate and financial manipulation of campaign populism and identity politics in service to the reigning big-money bankrollers and their global empire. The nation's first Black president advanced Wall Street's control of Washington and the related imperial agenda of the 'Pentagon System' more effectively than stiff and wealthy white Republicans like John McCain or Mitt Romney could have done. The reigning U.S. system of corporate and imperial "inverted totalitarianism" (Wolin) received a deadly, fake-democratic re-branding. The underlying "rightward drift" sharpened, fed by a widespread sense of popular abandonment and betrayal, which Republicans promptly exploited as the Democrats depressed and demobilized their own purported popular base.

HOW FASCIST LIARS GET TO LOOK "AUTHENTIC"

What does any of this have to do with the rise of Donald Trump? Quite a bit. In his important 2018 book *How Fascism Works: The Politics of Us and Them,* philosophy professor Jason Stanley demonstrated how Trump and a broad range of far-right political leaders around the world were using and subverting "democratic" electoral politics to gain power. Many American Democrats certainly read Stanley's book with a sense of self-satisfied validation over his description of Trump and his party as fascists. This was a bad mistake. Not content merely to describe fascist politics, Stanley also explained the prerequisites essential to its success. Fascism's taproot, Stanley argued, was harsh socio-economic disparity:

> Ever since Plato and Aristotle wrote on the topic, political theorists have known that democracy cannot flourish on soil poisoned by inequality…the resentments bred by such divisions are tempting targets for demagogues… Dramatic inequality poses a mortal danger to the shared reality required for a healthy liberal democracy…[such] inequality breeds delusions that mask reality, undermining the possibility of joint deliberation to sole society's divisions (pp.76–77)…

> Under conditions of stark economic inequality, when the benefits of liberal education, and the exposure to diverse cultures and norms are available only to the wealthy few, liberal tolerance can be smoothly represented as elite privilege. Stark economic inequality creates conditions richly conducive to fascist demagoguery. It is a fantasy to

> think that liberal democratic norms can flourish under such
> conditions. (p. 185)

Particularly perceptive is Stanley's intimate reflection on how the political culture of pseudo-democratic duplicity and disingenuousness that is generated by modern capitalist inequality and plutocracy creates space for fascist-style politicians who "appear to be sincere" and "signal authenticity" by "standing for division and conflict without apology." As Stanley writes, "Such a candidate might openly side with Christians over Muslims and atheists, or native-born [white] Americans over immigrants, or whites over blacks…They might openly and brazenly lie…[and] signal authenticity by openly and explicitly rejecting what are presumed to be sacrosanct political values….Such politicians," Stanley argues, come off to many jaded voters as "a breath of fresh air in a political culture that seems dominated by real and imagined hypocrisy." Fascist politicos' "open rejection of democratic values" is "taken as political bravery, as a signal of authenticity."

That describes the jaded conditions that opened the door to malevolent far-right figures at home and abroad. The opening is provided by neo-"liberals" (in the U.S) and neoliberal social democrats and "socialists" (in Europe and elsewhere) whose claims to speak on behalf of the popular majority and democracy are repeatedly discredited by an underlying commitment to capitalist social hierarchies and oppression structures.

He did not say so, but Stanley surely knew that the corporate ("neoliberal") Democratic Party of the late 20th and early 21st centuries partnered with Republicans to create a New Gilded Age characterized by extreme class disparity, which has further undermined democracy and encouraged intolerance among a large swath of Americans. For decades, the Democrats have participated in the richly bipartisan crafting of plutocratic policies that have shifted wealth and income so far upward that three absurdly rich people (Bill Gates, Warren Buffett, and Jeff Bezos) now possess as much combined wealth as the poorest half of

Americans. By the end of Obama's second term in office, the top tenth of the upper One Percent had accumulated as much wealth as the nation's bottom ninety percent.

This savage inequality has been administered with daunting doses of soul-numbing hypocrisy within the Democratic Party as well as within the Republican Party. Both parties/fundraising platforms have embodied the cold and disingenuous "manipulation of populism by elitism" that Christopher Hitchens aptly called, in a 1999 study of Bill and Hillary Clinton, "the essence of American politics." Obama staffed his White House with representatives from the banking and corporate world and crafted policy in dutiful accord with the dictates of the nation's big financial institutions. So had Bill Clinton, whose key campaign watchwords of "hope" and "change" as well as his strategies of running on "the economy, stupid" and the promise of universal health care were stealthily pilfered by Obama in 2007 and 2008.

Then came Hillary Clinton's 2016 Goldman Sachs campaign, poisoned by the disconnect between her transparent allegiance to the nation's top financial institutions and her admittedly tepid populist pretense. Clinton's pretense was undermined further when she got caught calling Trump's "flyover country" Republican supporters a "basket of" racist and sexist "deplorables" in a sneering commentary she delivered to rich Manhattan campaign donors. (Here, Clinton gave Trump something like the campaign gift that Romney provided Obama in 2012, when the Republican contender was heard telling rich donors that forty-seven percent of the country were lazy moochers).

This kind of disingenuous corporate-driven Democratic politics did a great deal to bring widely hated Republicans into the White House in both 2001 and 2017. The elitist fake-progressivism of neo-Weimar-liberals like the Clintons, Al Gore, and Barack Obama opened the door for hideous monsters like George W. Bush (who claimed to believe that God told him to invade Iraq) and the more genuinely fascistic Trump. These transparently inauthentic liberals made Republican candidates look comparatively authentic and served, too, to demobilize the Democrats' more authentically progressive popular base—the latter a point which Stanley misses. In fact, deeply uninspired by Hillary Clinton's tepid, elitist, and dismissive campaign, non-voting on the part of traditionally Democratic segments of the electorate was more critical to Trump's victory than any imagined big wave of white working-class Trump votes.

True, no U.S. president has ever lied as voluminously and pathologically as the fascist Trump. A brazen practitioner of the totalitarian "permanent lie" (which Hannah Arendt defined as "the consistent and total substitution of lies for factual truth"), Trump is off the historical charts when it comes to barefaced falsification. Still, the totalitarian would not have gotten into office without the more sophisticated establishmentarian disingenuousness of the party Wolin rightly called the "Inauthentic Opposition"—the dismal, demobilizing, depressing, and dollar-drenched Democrats.

THE CURSE OF BIGNESS

The Inauthentic Opposition party, it should be noted, has done nothing neither in nor out of the White House to address another critical factor in the rise of authoritarian right-wing politics: extreme economic concentration, or what the Supreme Court Justice Louis Brandeis called "the curse of bigness." Under Clinton and Obama as well as under Reagan, the Bushes, and Trump, the U.S., writes Columbia law professor Tim Wu, has:

> Weaken[ed] the laws—the antitrust laws that are meant to resist the concentration of economic power in the United States and around the world...we have recklessly chosen to tolerate global monopolies and oligopolies in finance, media, airlines, telecommunications and elsewhere, to say nothing of the growing size and power of the major technology platforms. In so doing, we have cast aside the safeguards that were supposed to protect democracy against

> a dangerous marriage of private and public power …[and
> thereby fueled anger on the part of] citizens who lost
> almost any influence over economic policy and by exten-
> sion, their lives…Their powerlessness is brewing a powerful
> feeling of outrage.[3]

The pervasive sense of powerlessness and resulting rage are sentiments that fascist politicos like Steve Bannon, Donald Trump, Viktor Orban, Jair Bolsonaro, and others around the world have powerfully exploited and misdirected against immigrants, ethnic and racial minorities, liberals, the left (fascists typically conflate the last two categories), urban professionals, and other convenient targets (including independent judicial officials, reporters, academics, and other dangerous relics of "democracy") while working for the very same structures of concentrated corporate wealth and power that fuel the mass middle-class indignation.

THE OLIGARCHS THAT MATTERED MOST IN 2016

All these forces came to a head in November of 2016, when corporate Democrat and imperialist Hillary Clinton, who Obama preferred as his successor over the progressive-populist Bernie Sanders, was defeated by Trump, the candidate who Obama knew to be a "fascist." Anyone whose sole news sources were MSNBC, CNN, and other corporate-Democratic and Obama-worshipping media venues might have thought that Trump's victory came courtesy of "oligarchs," a vaguely coded reference to Russian oligarchs and their supposedly decisive interference in the United States' purportedly grand, democratic electoral process. In reality, however, the oligarchs who mattered most in the election's outcome were American ones: the corporate and high finance election investors whose monetary largesse encouraged the conservative corporate Democratic nominee Hillary Clinton to mount a depressingly dull and centrist campaign that said remarkably little on policy. Despite her own widespread unpopularity in the first place, Clinton ran almost completely on candidate character.

Trump, by contrast, used his own money, massive free corporate media coverage, and critical financial support from far-right oligarchs like casino mogul Sheldon Adelson and hedge fund wizard Robert Mercer to mount a "reactionary populist" (neofascistic) campaign that combined white nationalism and sexism with dripping denunciations of Wall Street, Goldman Sachs, and globalization, plus pledges of allegiance to the "forgotten" American working class. "In striking contrast to every other Republican presidential nominee since 1936," the expert campaign finance researcher Thomas Ferguson noted, Trump "attacked globalization, free trade, international financiers, Wall Street, and even Goldman Sachs….He even criticized the 'carried interest' tax break beloved by high finance." However disingenuous and laced with authoritarian racism, sexism, and nativism it may have been, Trump's story of elite-manipulated populism was popular with a considerable portion of the electorate, thanks to the widespread economic insecurity that had spread among the populace during the transparently bipartisan New Gilded Age and with special poignancy in the wake of the Great Recession. He would become the first Republican presidential nominee in memory to outperform his Democratic opponent with small (middle-class and working-class) donors.

WE'RE WORSE OFF THAN BEFORE

But the 2016 election's tragic outcome wasn't just about Hillary Clinton, the Democratic National Committee, their big money backers, the Electoral College, or racist and partisan voter suppression in battleground states. It was also about Obama's center-right, corporate presidency, which left masses of American citizens, including no small number of Black Americans, wondering why they should cast another presidential ballot after Obama's supposedly "transformational" presidency, which was

full of such remarkable outward promise and symbolic progress—
the first Black president in the land of Black chattel slavery—and
yet yielded so few concrete social and material gains for ordinary
Americans.

"What matters," the great Black revolutionary Frantz Fanon
once wrote, "is not so much the color of your skin as the power
you serve and the millions you betray." The millions of Americans
who felt betrayed by the corporate globalist Obama included
many Black voters who had been initially inspired by Obama's
rise. In a memorable post-election *New York Times* report on
widespread Black non-voting in Milwaukee (the most populous
city in the critically contested state of Wisconsin) during the 2016
election, reporter Sabrina Tavernise reflected on her visit to the
heavily segregated city's Black North Side:

> At Upper Cutz, a bustling barbershop in a green-trimmed
> wooden house, talk of politics inevitably comes back to
> one man: Barack Obama. Mr. Obama's elections infused
> many here with a feeling of connection to national politics
> they had never before experienced. But their lives have not
> gotten appreciably better, and sourness has set in.

> "We went to the beach," said Maanaan Sabir, 38, owner of
> the Juice Kitchen, a brightly painted shop a few blocks
> down West North Avenue, using a metaphor to describe the
> emotion after Mr. Obama's election. "And then eight years
> happened."

> All four barbers had voted for Mr. Obama. But only two
> could muster the enthusiasm to vote this time. And even
> then, it was a sort of protest. One wrote in Mrs. Clinton's
> Democratic opponent, Senator Bernie Sanders of Vermont.
> The other wrote in himself.

> "I'm so numb," said John Toney, 45, who had written in
> Mr. Sanders. He said no president in his lifetime had done
> anything to improve the lives of black people, including Mr.
> Obama, whom he voted for twice. "It's like I should have
> known this would happen. We're worse off than before.'"

> Mr. Fleming, 47, who has been trimming hair, beards
> and mustaches for 30 years, had hoped his small business
> would get easier to run. But it hasn't…"Give us loans, or a
> 401(k)," he said…His biggest issue was health insurance. Mr.
> Fleming lost his coverage after his divorce three years ago
> and has struggled to find a policy he could afford. He finally
> found one, which starts Monday but costs too much at $300
> a month. "Ain't none of this been working," he said. He did
> not vote.

There's every reason to think that Ms. Tavernise could have found much the same story in the Black communities of other large cities in the battleground states that put Trump over the top against the dismal, dollar-drenched Democrats: Detroit and Flint in Michigan, Cincinnati and Cleveland in Ohio, Pittsburgh and Philadelphia in Pennsylvania, Raleigh and Charlotte in North Carolina, Miami, Tampa and Orlando in Florida. By the fifth year of Obama's presidency, U.S. Black households' median net worth had fallen to one-thirteenth of the median wealth of U.S. white households. This helped generate a sense of futility about voting among Black citizens—a sense that contributed significantly to Clinton's failure to re-create the electoral coalition that elected Obama in 2008 and 2012. Talk about voter suppression! In this case, the Democrats imposed it on themselves.

ABOVE THE FRAY

Things might have turned out differently had Obama not been sanctimoniously insistent as president on striving to stay "above the fray" of partisan politics. Even as Tea Party and other Republicans relentlessly criticized and opposed his every policy in often racist and neo-McCarthyite ways that strongly anticipated and informed the vicious 2015–16 Trump campaign, Obama refused, in the words of the historian Julian Zelezer, "to get… down and dirty in the muck of partisan politics." By Zelezer's account, Obama as president "declined to enter into bare-knuckled combat with Tea Party Republicans …Even as he faced a congressional GOP that would not vote for a stimulus bill in the worst part of a recession, and that made spurious accusations [that] he was not born in the United States, Obama stuck to his belief that compromise was possible and that reasoned dialogue could work." As Zelizer reflected in March of 2018, post-president Obama's refusal to strongly criticize and otherwise engage Trump "replicates the same mistake Obama made when he backed away from several tough fights with the GOP hoping his restraint would tone things down. It didn't." The Republicans continued to rail in white-nationalist rage against the nation's first Black president, Obama's reticence to fight in the partisan trenches meant that "Democrats didn't has as much to work with on the campaign trail."[4] This is a cogent point even if the centrist Zelizer is far too enthusiastic about the imperial and corporatist Obama policies that the he admonishes Obama for not boasting enough about.

PASSING ON THE IMPERIAL, MILITARY, AND AUTHORITARIAN POLICE-STATE BATON

There's another, far more direct sense in which Obama deserves to wear the Weimar Germany von Hindenburg cloak. The disgraced historical robe fits not just in regard to how the forty-fourth president and his fellow corporate Democrats opened the door for a fascistic takeover of the White House, but also in reference to the ways in which Obama directly passed the authoritarian, imperial, military, police-state and, by the way, eco-cidal baton—handed to him by Bill Clinton and two George Bushes—on to Trump.

As Noam Chomsky observed in May of 2017, Obama "punished more whistle-blowers than all previous presidents combined." The Obama administration also repeatedly defended George W. Bush's position on the indefinite detention of alleged "terrorists," maintaining that prisoners (U.S.-Americans included) in the U.S.-led global "war on [on] terror" were not entitled to *habeas corpus* or protection from torture or execution. With drones and Special Forces, Obama carried overseas assassinations—the execution, even of U.S. citizens, without trial or even formal charges—to new levels.

Regarding Obama's expanded global drone assassination program, Chomsky noted that "the [Obama] Justice Department explained that the constitutional guarantee of due process, tracing to Magna Carta, is now satisfied by internal deliberations in the executive branch alone. The constitutional lawyer in the White House agreed. King John (1199–1216) might have nodded with satisfaction."

"The system is outrageous," Refuse Fascism protesters have chanted under Trump, "they put our [immigrant] kids in cages." Obama has had nothing to say about this horrific crime, in part because he himself was a record-setting "deporter in chief" of Mexican and Central-American immigrants. Additionally, as the Associated Press reported last year, "Obama held children in temporary, ill-equipped facilities and built a large center in McAllen, Texas, that is used now. Democrats routinely and inaccurately blame Trump for creating 'cages' for children. They are actually referring to chain-link fencing inside the McAllen center—Obama's creation."[5]

There are many other examples of terrible policies, practices, and models of authoritarian indifference to democracy and human suffering that the Obama White House transmitted to the Trump administration.

Before Trump pulled out of the Paris Climate Accord, for example, Obama almost singlehandedly wrecked efforts at comprehensive and binding global carbon emission limits at the 2009 United Nations Climate Change Conference in Copenhagen, Denmark.

Before Trump offensively threw paper towels at Hurricane Maria's victims in Puerto Rico, President Obama ostentatiously downplayed Flint, Michigan's racist water crisis by drinking a sip of filtered Flint water in a sickening publicity stunt.

Obama initiated the reckless and ominous $1 trillion "upgrade" and "modernization" of the exterminist nuclear weapons arsenal that the "feral animal" Trump has had at his horrifying disposal since taking office.[6]

Concerned about the horrific anti-environmental, science-denying, anti-climate agenda of the Trump White House? You should be. But it is also important to recall what a tuxedo-clad Barack Obama had to say to an audience of rich Texans, mainly oil investors, at Rice University's Baker Institute in November of 2018: "American energy production… went up every year I was president. And… suddenly America's like the biggest oil producer. That was me, people." This was no false boast: Obama signed off on dramatic expansions of American gas and oil drilling, including the environmentally disastrous practice of hydraulic fracturing ("fracking").

Thanks, Obama!

A bracing *Intercept* article published three days after Trump's election bore the frightening and accurate title "Commander-in-Chief Donald Trump Will Have Terrifying Powers. Thanks Obama." As Alex Emmons explained, Obama implemented, oversaw, used, and was now set to bequeath to the malignant Trump "presidential powers that have never been more expansive and unchecked," including the following:

- "An unaccountable drone program"
- The torture prison at Guantanamo Bay
- A giant FBI, with 35,000 employees, "a network of 15,000 paid informants" and "a record of spying on mosques and activists"
- The "NSA's surveillance empire" that was "ubiquitous and governed by arcane rules, most of which remain secret"

- "Bombing campaigns in seven Muslim countries"
- "The de facto ability to declare war unilaterally"
- "A massive nuclear arsenal—much of which is on hair-trigger alert"
- A record-setting immigrant detention and deportation program, with "hundreds of thousands of immigrants in detention centers" and young children "force[d]..to appear before immigration judges without a lawyer"
- "A Justice Department that has waged an unprecedented war on press freedom"

Emmons also offered some chilling reflections on the chilling authoritarian powers Obama was set to pass off to a man who top Democrats had for months been reasonably calling deranged and dangerous. His observations merit lengthy quotation:

> Caught off-guard by Hillary Clinton's election defeat, Democrats who defended these powers under President Obama may suddenly be having second thoughts as the White House gets handed over to a man they described— with good reason—as "unhinged," and "dangerously unfit."
>
> In the years after the 9/11 terror attacks, Vice President Dick Cheney and his legal adviser David Addington dramatically expanded the powers of the presidency, asserting the unilateral right in wartime to ignore legal limits on things like torture and government eavesdropping. Congressional Democrats generally caved but made a few efforts to push back.

The Democrats went silent on executive overreach when Obama was elected, however.

> When the *New York Times* revealed Bush's warrantless wiretapping program in 2005, 60 percent of registered Democrats thought the program was "unacceptable." But after NSA whistleblower Edward Snowden revealed a dramatically larger surveillance apparatus in 2013, a 61 percent

of Democrats said the opposite—presumably because they trusted the man in charge.

After eight years of trusting the President with expanding military power, liberals must now reckon with the fact that Obama will pass the same capabilities to a man who has proposed killing terrorists' innocent family members, who has said he would do "a hell of a lot worse than waterboarding," and who has suggested dipping bullets in pigs' blood is sound counterterrorism strategy.

And most of the paltry few legal limitations that regulate the security state could easily be repealed by a President Trump.

In 2013, Obama's Justice Department seized the phone records from three Associated Press bureaus to uncover the source for a story. Obama also waged a seven-year legal campaign against *New York Times* reporter James Risen, threatening him with prison if he did not reveal his source for a story about a botched CIA operation. The prosecutors dropped the request at the last minute.

The legacy of that system is now passing into the hands of someone who has made a show of his contempt for the media. During his campaign, Trump repeatedly incited crowds against reporters, threatened publications with defamation lawsuits, and expressed his desire to "open up those libel laws."

President Obama has spent much of his time as commander in chief expanding his own military power, while convincing courts not to limit his detention, surveillance, and assassination capabilities. Most of the new constraints on the security state during the Obama years were self-imposed, and could easily be revoked.

Recall the absolute powers that Germany's Weimar President Paul Von Hindenburg handed off to Adolph Hitler, the Chancellor he appointed in early 1933: "The Constitution of the German Reich is suspended until further notice. It is therefore permissible to restrict the rights of personal freedom [*habeas corpus*], freedom of (opinion) expression, including the freedom of the press, the freedom to organize and assemble, the privacy of postal, telegraphic and telephonic communications. Warrants for House searches, orders for confiscations as well as restrictions on property, are also permissible beyond the legal limits otherwise prescribed."

"On the face of it," *The Nation*'s Jeet Heer wrote in mid-July of this year, it was "illegal and unconstitutional" for Trump's federal officers to sweep up social justice and civil rights protesters into unmarked marked cars in Portland. But "it's possible," Heer added, "that they are acting under the 2011 National Defense Authorization Act, signed by Barack Obama, which legalized the detention of Americans suspected of being terrorists. If so, then the War on Terrorism has truly come home."

BLAMING BLACK VICTIMS OF RACISM

Given Obama's much ballyhooed status as the nation's first Black president, one of the models of presidential conduct that Obama helped pass on to the racist Trump is profoundly ironic: a tendency to downplay the role of systemic racism and to emphasize the role of Black personal and cultural responsibility in the creation of the nation's stark racial inequalities. As the brilliant Black scholar William A. Darity, Jr. noted in an incisive December 2016 essay titled "How Barack Obama Failed Black Americans," President Obama trafficked heavily in the culturally white-supremacist claim that Blacks' economic difficulties were largely the result of Blacks' own "self-defeating or dysfunction-al behavior." In one of many examples of this recurrent Obama narrative, Obama told the 2013 graduates of historically Black Morehouse College that young Black men had "no excuses," and placed blame for Black difficulties in America at the feet of absen-tee fathers.

Darity wrote with barely concealed disgust about what he had seen and heard from a Black president who refused to advance policy solutions to the numerous and interrelated barriers to

Black advancement and equality, barriers which were upheld by the nation's deeply embedded structural and institutional racism:

> It has been damaging to have Barack Obama, a black man speaking from the authoritative platform of the presidency, reinforce the widely held belief that racial inequality in the United States is, in large measure, the direct responsibility of black folk. This has been the deal breaker for me: not merely a silence on white physical and emotional violence directed against black Americans, but the denial of the centrality of American racism in explaining sustained black-white disparity.

Darity noted the deep irony of the one and only Obama program designed specifically for Black Americans—a program rooted in the idea that racial disparity is largely about Black behavior:

> There is one major initiative that the Obama administration has inaugurated that is black-specific, but it is the exception that proves the rule. It exposes all the issues at play. My Brother's Keeper is a program premised on the view that young black men constitute a social problem and need interventions that will alter their outlook and actions. The focus is on reforming young men rather than directly increasing the resources possessed by them and their families and removing the constraints they face. Again, the underlying ideological motivation is the belief in black cultural deficiency, and, again, this type of initiative is another expression of failure to pursue bold policies that confront the fundamental causes of racial disparity in American society.[7]

Obama's failure to fight meaningfully for Black equality and racial justice beyond the symbolic fact of his own technically Black presence in the White House was all the more depressing in light of the unpleasant fact that his simple presence sparked a white racist backlash that could be counted on to target Black Americans who did not share the Obamas' elevated economic status and protections. Obama did nothing, or close to it, to advance or protect Black Americans while setting them up for intensified hatred and assault from whites who sadly but predictably took Obama's presidency to mean that Blacks and other non-whites were "taking over the country." That was an absurd belief that Donald Trump was more than happy to fan and exploit.

"HE PUT IN HIS EIGHT YEARS OF SERVICE" (TO RICH WHITES)

Obama's role in the creation of the Trump presidency has been missed even by some who have properly criticized his quiescence on the Trump presidency from the portside. Read, for instance, the opening paragraph of David Magary's 2020 rant, "Where the Hell is Barack Obama?" (quoted at length in the previous chapter):

> My patience with Barack Obama's patience is at an end. Since leaving office at the beginning of 2017, the former president made it his priority to lay low. Under normal circumstances, no one could begrudge him that choice. He had just been president for eight years. He was tired. His family was tired. He had more than earned the right to fuck off and enjoy himself, especially given the endless stream of bullshit he had to endure as our first black president…. These are far beyond normal circumstances and he no longer has that right.

What Magary failed to grasp here was that Trump's "abnormal" and apocalyptic presidency was to no small extent Obama's production.

The same omission was evident in a June 2018 *The Root* article in which the bourgeois identitarian Monique Judge argued that it was essentially racist for anyone to simultaneously be white and think it was incumbent on Obama to speak up against the Trump nightmare. "Obama," Judge actually titled her essay, "Doesn't Owe This Country Shit." By Judge's judgement:

> Obama is doing exactly what he wants, and there is nothing
> wrong with that. He spent eight years serving the will of the
> American people. Now he gets to do what Barack wants....
> His life is about him. We don't own him. We aren't entitled
> to him. *You* don't own him. *You* aren't entitled to him. The
> days of America benefiting off the free labor of black folks
> are long over. Obama did his time. He put in his eight years
> of service in the White House. He endured the criticism.
> He withstood the abuse lobbed at his wife and daughters.
> He smiled and waved and hugged and kissed babies and
> was the picture of dignity the entire time he was in office.
> He did his time, and he moved on. When he left, America
> voted in an ignorant, xenophobic, racist egomaniac who has
> spent his entire time in office doing everything in his power
> to tear down Obama's legacy. And this country is sitting by
> and letting him do it. Obama is supposed to care about this
> country? Man, fuck this country. Obama doesn't owe this
> country shit.

Judge's bitter assessment neglected to mention that Obama enjoys a $200,000 lifetime pension, free taxpayer-funded travel and business expenses, and the right to cash in on his many years of policymaking on behalf of the rich by becoming fabulously wealthy himself. As Judge also failed to note, Obama spent his eight years in the White House not "serving the will of the American people," but serving the will of the nation's unelected and interrelated dictatorships of money and empire in ways that helped open the door and hand the key of fascistic rule to Trump. The following chapter turns to the rewards that ex-president Obama has reaped for his service to the American ruling class— compensation granted and enjoyed as the nation descended into the fascist apocalypse he told his staffers and David Remnick wasn't happening after Trump was elected.

It seems that no small portion of American "democracy" was already "falling apart" before Trump took charge. And Obama, along with his predecessors, had much to do with the demolition project that set the stage for Trump. Thanks, Obama!

ENDNOTES

1. David Cay Johnson, "November Election: Don't Count on Trump Yet," *D.C. Report,* June 17, 2020, https://www.dcreport.org/2020/06/17/dont-count-out-trump-yet/?fbclid=IwAR3HWB5Nja2-OeE-YgI7WX-K3ILlywmS6ocv6Cu2msnbtU7P1UwpMwK5ciF8

2. Ian Schwartz, "Obama Warning Compares Untended Democracy to Nazi Germany," *Real Clear Politics,* December 8, 2017, https://www.realclearpolitics.com/video/2017/12/08/obama_warning_compares_untended_democracy_to_nazi_germany.html

3. Tim Wu, "Be Afraid of Economic 'Bigness.' Be Very Afraid," *New York Times*, November 10, 2018

4. Julian Zelizer, "Where is Barack Obama? ," *The Atlantic*, March 19, 2018.

5. Hope Yen and Calvin Woodward, "AP Fact Check: Obama is a Silent Partner in Trump's Boasts," *AP News,* June 23, 2019, https://apnews.com/fdfbafe-1f2784a759bc7c3a8e8ddbcab

6. Barry Blechman, "A Trillion-Dollar Nuclear Weapon Modernization is Unnecessary," *New York Times,* October 26, 2016, https://www.nytimes.com/roomfordebate/2016/10/26/a-nuclear-arsenal-upgrade/a-trillion-dollar-nuclear-weapon-modernization-is-unnecessary

7. William A. Darity, Jr., "How Barack Obama Failed Black Americans," *The Atlantic,* December 22, 2016, https://www.theatlantic.com/politics/archive/2016/12/how-barack-obama-failed-black-americans/511358/?fbclid=IwAR2EO1eC6Tl4CxxEh5wahPVGC1y7mr_AsJNAAlnFQkJmndDPbntfq-Ty8oI

CHAPTER 4
Playing and Cashing In

The democratic socialist Dr. Martin Luther King, Jr., whose bust sat behind Barack Obama's Oval Office desk, would no more have approved of Obama's retirement than he would have admired Obama's corporate and imperial presidency. King would have been offended by Obama's general reticence to combat Trump's open white nationalism and mockery of the nation's alleged democratic values.

"He who passively accepts evil," King once said, "is as much involved in it as he who helps to perpetrate it. He who accepts evil without protesting against it is really cooperating with it."

"There comes a time," King also remarked, "when silence is betrayal."

"In the end," King added, "we will remember not the words of our enemies but the silence of our friends."

King would also be displeased with Obama's post-presidential determination to profit from his many years of service to the rich and powerful while soaking up the pleasures of wealth and celebrity. Cashing in on fame was something King steadfastly refused to do. When he was notified in 1964 that he had won the Nobel Peace Prize, as David Garrow notes in *Bearing the Cross*, his Pulitzer Prize-winning biography of King, the Civil Rights icon announced that he would turn over the prize money of $54,123 to the struggle for Black equality and social justice. Much to the chagrin of his long-suffering wife, King followed through with his pledge. He never stopped fighting against what he called the "triple evils that are interrelated"—racism (deeply understood), poverty (class inequality and capitalism), and militarism-imperialism. And he pushed himself so hard in his final years that he died as a martyr with the body of a much older man.

Obama has taken a different approach, one that is consistent with his earlier history, and also consistent with the findings and argument of a remarkable, under-read study by the University of Kentucky political historian Ron Formisano. In Formisano's highly detailed but under-appreciated account in *American Oligarchy: The Permanence of the Political Class* (2017), U.S. politics and policy are under the control of a "permanent political class"—a "networked layer of high-income people," including congressional representatives (half of whom are millionaires), elected officials, campaign funders, lobbyists, consultants, appointed bureaucrats, pollsters, celebrity television journalists, university presidents, and executives at well-funded nonprofit institutions. This "permanent political class," Formisano finds, is taking the nation "beyond [mere] plutocracy" into "the hegemony of an aristocracy of inherited wealth."

Formisano documents the top concern of politicians and the politically connected in the age of American oligarchy: watching out "for me and mine." Over the years, elected officials have become adept at monetizing their public service, turning years of dutiful obedience to the possessing classes while in "public office" into ladders on which they climb into the nation's oligarchy. "Public service" has become an avenue to private wealth for the permanent political class, their family members, and friends.

Obama, who campaigned in 2007 and 2008 touting his middle class-status and criticizing the wealthy Few (while being pushed left by his more progressive and populist-sounding fellow candidate John Edwards) has been no exception to Formisano's formulations. His ruling class-sponsored upward climb, combined with egregious displays of selfish pleasure-taking alongside flashy plutocrats and celebrities, has been, to say the least, unseemly. Moreover, Obama's retirement activities serve as evidence of the ostentatious rewards received in return for loyalty to the nation's un-elected dictatorship of money.

Where has Obama been as Trump has plundered, wreaked havoc, and set new records for smashing the norms of U.S. presidential conduct? Part of the answer is that he's been violating post-presidential norms himself by playing with the rich and famous, basking in their grotesquely opulent lifestyles of leisure.

A *Reuters* report in early February 2017 bore the provocative headline "Obama Kiteboards in Caribbean with Billionaire Richard Branson." As *Reuters* informed its readers:

> Former U.S. president Barack Obama is trying some new and dangerous water sports that the Hawaii native had to miss out on for safety reasons while serving in the White House.
>
> Obama, whose eight years as president ended last month when he was succeeded by Donald Trump, learned to kiteboard while vacationing last week on a Caribbean island owned by British billionaire and adventurer Sir Richard Branson, who published an account of their trip…
>
> Photographs and video on the website of Branson's Virgin Group show the former president, a life-long surfer, figuring out the increasingly popular sport in which people ride a board while being pulled behind a kite.
>
> "Being the former president of America, there was lots of security around, but Barack was able to really relax and get into it," Branson wrote.
>
> Obama and his wife, Michelle, were spotted last week in the British Virgin Islands, and people posted photos of them on social media. Branson owns 120-acre (48-hectare) Moskito Island, which is part of the archipelago.
>
> ….According to Branson, Obama studied the pastime for two days and flew a kite from the beach, "as if going back to being a child again," before heading out into the waves.
>
> Branson was trying to learn a similar sport, foilboarding, which uses a modified board that rises a few feet above the water. He wrote that he challenged the ex-president over which of them would succeed first.

> Obama triumphed, he said, by kiteboarding for 100 meters (328 feet).
>
> "After all he has done for the world, I couldn't begrudge him his well-deserved win," Branson wrote.[1]

Obama was apparently quite chummy with Branson, the British billionaire airline mogul who was leading the charge for the privatization of the United Kingdom's National Health Service. A photograph Branson posted online showed the British oligarch and Obama pretending to fight each other. Perhaps, between bouts and kiteboarding outings, they discussed how to make the U.K.'s healthcare system more capitalist and less socialist, using Obama's Affordable Care Act, and its happy relationships between the government and private health insurance and drug companies, as a model.

As *Reuters* neglected to mention, the ocean waters in which Obama played with Branson were extraordinarily warm, helping to set the stage for the hurricanes to which Trump would respond so poorly, thanks at least in some small part to Obama's presidential efforts on behalf of U.S. oil and gas corporations.

From a whirlwind trip around the Caribbean, it was off for a month to French Polynesia for a month of relaxation on a resort island formerly owned by Hollywood superstar Marlon Brando. The Obamas took a break from their "quiet island life" to enjoy a Pacific cruise and lunch with Oprah Winfrey, Tom Hanks, and Bruce Springsteen on a $300 million luxury yacht owned by recording mogul David Geffen. A breathless account of this star-studded dining and yachting adventure appeared in London's *Daily Mail*:

> They've spent the last month quietly recuperating in French Polynesia since leaving the White House earlier this year. But Barack and Michelle Obama interrupted the quiet island life they've become accustomed to this weekend with a star-studded jaunt out to sea. The former First Couple joined Bruce Springsteen Tom Hanks and their wives on

music mogul David Geffen's superyacht Rising Sun on Friday, making quite the splash as they arrived at the vessel off the island of Mo'orea in a spruced up speedboat.

Once on board, the Obamas played tourists, posing romantically on the upper deck while they had their photograph taken. Michelle and Barack Obama posed for a photograph on the upper deck of billionaire music mogul David Geffen's superyacht on Friday as the former First Couple carried on their Tahitian vacation off the island of Mo'orea.

The former president was also seen taking photographs of Michelle as she posed alone. Out of sight were…Hanks and Springsteen, both of whom are considered friends by the Obamas. Both are also close with Geffen, a billionaire music mogul who prides himself on the famous company he keeps on board his $300 million yacht.

Springsteen and Hanks are regular guests while Mariah Carey, James Packer, Leonardo di Caprio and Steven Spielberg have also graced its deck.

Oprah, another friend of the billionaire's, was rumored by local media to have also been on board but was not spotted as the group posed for photographs.

The stunning 454ft-long yacht was built for Oracle CEO Larry Ellison and bought by Geffen in 2010.[2]

"The Weinstein Company" was the film company owned by the soon-to-be disgraced rapist and Hollywood mogul Harvey Weinstein, whose crimes would help spawn the Me Too movement.

Between the day he handed power over to Trump, who he knew to be a "fascist" and whose ascendancy he helped produce, and early April of 2017, Obama spent leisure time, at no small taxpayer expense, in Hawaii, Palm Springs, the Caribbean, and French Polynesia. The General Services Administration is required to provide former presidents with money to cover their business and travel expenses, so it's likely that U.S. taxpayers were saddled with at least a portion of their vacation costs.

Just how wealthy are the Obamas now? According to American University, CNN Money, and GoBankingRates, the Obamas' net worth has risen by a factor of more than thirty from when they entered the White House in 2009 (1.3 million dollars) to 2018 (at least 40 million dollars). This places them close to the top tenth of the upper One Percent.

Regular income is only a partial contributor to this wealth. (Obama received 400,000 dollars a year as president and is granted an annual pension of 200,000 dollars.) The lion's share of the Obamas' net worth has come from book contracts. By *Forbes*' calculations, Obama made 15.6 million dollars in advances and royalties from his books *The Audacity of Hope*, *Of Thee I Sing: A Letter to My Daughters*, and *Dreams From My Father*.

In 2017, Barack and Michelle Obama signed his-and-her book deals with Penguin Random House worth a combined 65 million dollars. Michelle Obama's ghostwritten memoir, *Becoming*, sold ten million copies, making it the nation's top bestseller. Mrs. Obama also sold twenty-five different types of merchandise marketed in connection with her book, including "Becoming" mugs priced at twenty dollars and candles retailing at thirty-five dollars each.

It's not just about books when it comes to lucrative media contracts for the forty-fourth president. In May of 2018, the Obamas signed a fifty million dollar production deal with Netflix. The deal awarded the Obamas the ability to produce films and series for the reigning online streaming service. "We are incredibly proud they have chosen to make Netflix the home for their formidable storytelling abilities," Netflix's chief content officer Ted Sarandos said in a news release. Sarandos failed to mention that he and his wife had raised more than half a million dollars for Obama as campaign finance bundlers in 2012—or that his wife, Nicole Avant, was appointed by Obama as ambassador to the Bahamas between 2009 and 2011.[3]

Then there's the big money accrued from public speaking, with Obama netting as much as 400,000 dollars for a single speech. According to the *New York Post* in a November 2018 report cleverly titled "The Obamas are 'Becoming' a Billion Dollar Brand," Obama "earned" 800,000 dollars for two speeches to Northern Trust Corporation and the Carlyle Group, a firm heavily invested in the nation's military-industrial complex, and a minimum of 1.2 million dollars for three talks to Wall Street firms in 2017. Obama got 400,000 dollars, too, for speaking at a Wall Street health care conference hosted by the financial services giant Cantor Fitzgerald, L.P.

Meanwhile, Michelle Obama has reportedly garnered 225,000 dollars per speaking appearance since leaving the White House. Tickets to her 2018 book tour at Brooklyn's Barclay's Center ranged from 307 dollars to 4,070 dollars.

By the estimation of academic researchers at American University, the Obamas can expect to make 242.5 million dollars over the rest of their lives.[4] They can be expected to rival the Clintons (who grossed 153 million dollars for 729 speeches, earning an average of 210,795 dollars per address between 2001 and 2016) as the wealthiest post-presidential couple in American history.

Not surprisingly, the post-presidential Obamas have been conspicuous spenders as well as super-opulent "earners." They have purchased an 8,200-square-foot mansion in Washington, DC, for 8.1 million dollars and a luxuriant home with thirty acres of land on Martha's Vineyard for 11.75 million dollars.

It's called getting paid for services rendered. As Obama knows very well, nothing says "show me the money" like "President of the United States" on your resume—especially when you spent your presidential terms serving the nation's unelected directorate of finance, whose representatives held key posts in your administration. Call it the Audacity of Sleaze and the Venality of Hope.

It's not just about the money and luxurious travel and dining, of course. Obama has spent much of his post-presidency indulging in his love for playing golf, as well as watching and commenting on mass spectator sports. Rumored to want part-ownership of a National Basketball Association franchise, Obama speaks regularly with NBA superstars LeBron James and Steph Curry. He and Michelle have been spotted at a Beyoncé concert.

ORWELLIAN LEGACY PROTECTION I: A "PRESIDENTIAL LIBRARY THAT ISN'T"

Obama is also heavily involved in the promoting and protecting his legacy. On May 3, 2017, one day after Trump's Department of Health and Human Services disclosed a plan to roll back regulations interpreting Obamacare's nondiscrimination provisions to protect transgendered people, Obama unveiled the plans for the $500 million Obama Presidential Library. "As the name would indicate," *Architectural Digest* reported, "a presidential library is a very special, almost sacred space. Its duty is to compile the many documents and artifacts of a president and his administration and present them to the public for greater clarity and discussion."[5] In reality, however, Obama's announcement and plan suggested something less than sober and honest historical reflection. On the day of the unveiling, Obama said he wanted his library to be a place that "looked forward, not backward, and [that] would provide a place to train future leaders." Consistent with the soft Orwellianism of that comment and with Obama's deep commitment to corporate neoliberal ideology, the *New York Times* reported in February of 2019 that Obama's "presidential library" wouldn't contain a library at all and that it would be privately managed by his own nonprofit foundation, making it the first modern "presidential library" not to be run by federal archival authorities:

> The Obama Presidential Library That Isn't

The Obama Presidential Center promises to be a presidential library like no other.

The four-building, 19-acre "working center for citizenship," set to be built in a public park on the South Side of Chicago, will include a 235-foot-high "museum tower," a two-story event space, an athletic center, a recording studio, a winter garden, even a sledding hill.

But the center, which will cost an estimated $500 million, will also differ from the complexes built by Barack Obama's predecessors in another way: It won't actually be a presidential library.

In a break with precedent, there will be no research library on site, and none of Mr. Obama's official presidential records. Instead, the Obama Foundation will pay to digitize the roughly 30 million pages of unclassified paper records from the administration so they can be made available online.

And the entire complex, including the museum chronicling Mr. Obama's presidency, will be run by the foundation, a private nonprofit entity, *rather than by the National Archives and Records Administration, the federal agency that administers the libraries and museums for all presidents going back to Herbert Hoover.* [Emphasis added][6]

... all indications initially pointed to a traditional Obama presidential library in Chicago. In late 2016, military convoys began shipping some 30 million pages of paper documents and 30,000 artifacts to a former furniture store in suburban Hoffman Estates, Ill.

In May 2017, when President Obama appeared in Chicago to unveil the design for the center, renderings included a 50,000-square-foot "Library Building." But the research facility and archives most people had assumed would be inside it had disappeared.

Obama's determination to digitize his archives, dispense with any notion of a library, and put his records under private control ought to send dystopian chills down the spine of historians, not to mention U.S. and world citizens. In George Orwell's classic novel *1984*, the dystopian superstate of Oceania is run by the fictional English Socialist Party, known in the Newspeak language of Oceania as Ingsoc. Ingsoc is led by a mysterious (and perhaps mythical) leader known as "Big Brother." The protagonist of the novel is Winston Smith, an editor in the Records Department at the governmental office Ministry of Truth, where he actively revises historical records to make the past conform to whatever Ingsoc wants it to be. One day he wakes up and thinks:

> Who controls the past, controls the future: who controls
> the present, controls the past... The mutability of the past
> is the central tenet of Ingsoc. Past events, it is argued, have
> no objective existence, but survive only in written records
> and in human memories. The past is whatever the records
> and the memories agree upon. And since the Party is in
> full control of all records, and in equally full control of the
> minds of its members, it follows that the past is whatever
> the Party chooses to make it.

Adding more insult and injury to insult and injury, Obama's "library that isn't" amounts to technical displacement for librarians and archivists, who would otherwise serve the institution as they do at other presidential libraries. It has also riled Chicago environmental and anti-gentrification activists[7] because its construction means the destruction of rich urban greenspace in Chicago's historic Jackson Park while fueling heightened property values in the nearby and very predominantly Black neighborhood of Woodlawn.

LEGACY PROTECTION II:
WRITING HIS OWN HISTORY, AT NO SMALL LENGTH

Perhaps Obama will enjoy privileged access to his own presidential records as he completes his third book on his favorite subject: himself. Obama's reportedly thousand-page-long memoir, which netted him more than 40 million dollars, should certainly be expected to provide a grand and narcissistic dive into his years of dedicated service to the American elite. In his epic 2017 biography of Obama, *Rising Star: The Making of Barack Obama*, which also spans more than one thousand pages, the distinguished historian David Garrow notes that a young Obama tried to beat historians to the punch by writing a deceptive, self-serving account of his own first three-and-a-half decades gracing the planet with his own "special qualities" (Obama's words). Based on careful historical fact-checking, Garrow takes to task Obama's 1995 autobiography *Dreams From My Father* and some later autobiographical reflections for numerous distortions and embellishments of the future president's history:

- inventing a nonexistent deep racial identity drama during Obama's early years in Hawaii, Indonesia, and Occidental College

- incorrectly portraying Obama as a "difference-maker" on his high school basketball team

- deceptively claiming that Obama had been an angry "thug" during high school

- deleting the Communist Party background of the Black "old poet" ("Frank," as in longtime Communist Party activist Frank Davis) who gave Obama advice as a teenager in Honolulu

- inaccurately claiming that Obama received a "full scholarship" to Occidental

- absurdly misrepresenting himself as a leader in the movement against South African apartheid at Occidental

- exaggerating Obama's involvement in anti-apartheid activism at Columbia University

- covering up evidence of Obama's enrollment in a Columbia course taught by a Marxist academic

- mispresenting the nature of Obama's work for the New York Public Interest Research Group (NYPIRG) at the City University of New York

- concocting a mythical and supposedly life-changing dialogue with a "black security guard" on Obama's first trip from New York City to begin community organizing work on the far South Side of Chicago

- falsely claiming that Obama converted to Christianity during his early years in Chicago

- largely writing Obama's white mother out of his history and over-playing the role of his father (Barack Obama. Sr.) in his life

- painting a "decidedly uncharitable portrait" of Obama's white maternal grandfather (Stanley Dunham), who did much to lovingly raise him

- falsely suggesting that Obama's maternal white grandmother was a racist

- unduly downplaying Obama's supreme enjoyment of his years at Harvard Law School

- coldly condensing his three top pre-marital girlfriends "into a single woman whose appearance in the book was fleeting indeed"

Garrow judges *Dreams* "a work of historical fiction," not a serious autobiography or memoir. We should expect much the same thing on historical steroids in Obama's forthcoming tome of a memoir, which will concentrate on his presidential years. To quote an old historical maxim, recently recycled by Trump's Attorney General William Barr (as justification for his decision to drop charges against Michael Flynn, Trump's former National Security Advisor), "history is written by the winners."

Slated to "earn" in excess of 240 million dollars and to enjoy a life of island hopping and celebrity socializing, Obama has ascended beyond the rank of simple political figure to celebrity status, something he seemed to long for throughout his life. Meanwhile, some islands are literally disappearing as sea levels rise because of the climate crisis, and the world is descending into ever-deepening social, political, economic, epidemiological, and environmental catastrophe. As he settles into his super-lucrative post-presidency life, Obama certainly deserves to be considered one of late capitalism's "winners." The preponderant majority of the country and species, however, find themselves on the other side of the ledger.

But, of course, consistent with Obama's Orwellian reference to his non-library focusing on "looking forward" and not "backward" (he said something similar when justifying his decision not to prosecute George W. Bush administration officials for engaging in torture), Obama's post-presidency has also been about politics in the present. The politics that interest Obama, however, are not of the variety that interested Dr. King, who Obama loves to quote and remake to suit his purposes. King's policies were about the needs and interests of the dispossessed and powerless. In contrast, Obama's politics are very carefully articulated, and largely limited to promoting the narrow electoral agenda of the nation's Inauthentic Opposition party—the corporate Democrats, who are currently trying to foist Obama's Vice President, Joe Biden, a highly flawed career politician, onto the nation and world as the solution to the Trumpenstein monster that Obama and his administration helped to create. It is to this depressing drama that the following chapter turns.

ENDNOTES

1. David Ingram, "Obama Kiteboards in Caribbean with Billionaire Richard Branson," *Reuters,* February 7, 2017, https://www.reuters.com/article/us-usa-obama-kiteboarding-idUSKBN15M1SP

2. Jennifer Smith, "A Picture Perfect Moment," *Daily Mail,* April 16, 2017, https://www.dailymail.co.uk/news/article-4416814/Barack-Michelle-Obama-pose-superyacht-Tahiti.html?fbclid=IwAR2UiFjNxJhS1GE3EsIq6hDTKJmXd_6B-P7a8APHuz5CUVJO-C67Gj5X9JqQ

3. Alex Pappas, "Obama's Netflix Deal Inked with Help from Bundler Buddy," *FOX News,* Mary 30, 2018, https://www.foxnews.com/politics/obamas-netflix-deal-inked-with-help-from-bundler-buddy

4. "How Presidents Make Their Millions," American University, January 9, 2017, https://onlinebusiness.american.edu/blog/presidents-net-worth/

5. Nick Mafi, "Barack Obama Unveils Bold Plans for His Presidential Library in Chicago," *Architectural Digest,* May 3, 2017, https://www.architecturaldigest.com/story/barack-obama-unveils-bold-plans-for-presidential-library-chicago

6. Jennifer Schuessler, "The Obama Presidential Library That Isn't," *New York Times,* February 20, 2019, https://www.nytimes.com/2019/02/20/arts/obama-presidential-center-library-national-archives-and-records-administration.html

7. Maya Rhodan, "Barack Obama Is Beloved in Chicago, But Activists Are Divided Over His Future Presidential Center," *TIME,* July 19, 2018, https://time.com/longform/barack-obama-chicago-presidential-center/

CHAPTER 5
Joe Biden? Thanks, Obama

The best way to protest is to vote. When you vote, you've got the power.
—Barack Obama, Urbana, Illinois. September 2018

We can disagree in the margins but the truth of the matter is it's all within our wheelhouse and nobody has to be punished. No one's standard of living will change, nothing would fundamentally change...I need you very badly...I won't let you down. I promise you.
—Joe Biden, speaking to wealthy donors in Manhattan, June 2019

Barack Obama wins the Democratic primary.
—Ryan Lizza, April 9, 2020

I'd vote for anybody over Trump, but did it have to be THIS anybody? Thanks to Obama, I guess it does.
—Drew Magary, April 14, 2020

"THE BEST WAY TO PROTEST IS TO VOTE"...

When an ABC television correspondent asked Vice President Dick Cheney about surveys demonstrating that the great majority of Americans opposed the war in Iraq, Cheney said, "So?"

"So—you don't care what the American people think?" the correspondent asked. "No," Cheney elaborated, "I think you cannot be blown off course by the fluctuations in public opinion polls."

Justifying Cheney's blunt remarks, White House spokesperson Dana Perino was later asked if the citizenry should have "input" on U.S. policy. "You had your input," Perino replied. "The American people have input every four years and that's the way our system is set up."

Noam Chomsky aptly summarized the core sentiment behind this remark: "Every four years the American people can choose between candidates whose views they reject and then they should shut up." As Chomsky noted at the time, citing relevant survey data from the Program on International Policy Attitudes, the preponderant majority of Americans disagreed. A remarkable 94 percent of U.S. citizens said that government leaders should pay attention to the views of the public between elections—a massive repudiation of the authoritarian notion that elections are the only time when the citizenry's opinion should have influence.

Cheney and Perino's comments were outrageous but they really aren't all that different from what Obama has had to say during his political career, including his post-presidential years. As Trump assaulted constitutional checks and balances and common decency during his first year in office, a financial services executive interviewing Obama at the Economic Club of Chicago Vladimir Lenin's question: "what is to be done?" After hemming and hawing about the unsteady but supposedly forward march of American democracy, Obama told his audience to "pay attention" and then "vote."

Ten months later, speaking to a largely college student audience 126 miles south of Chicago at the University of Illinois, Obama told young people that "the best way to protest is to vote. When you vote," Obama told young adults, "you've got the power."

In the spring of 2020, as hundreds of thousands of Americans took to the streets to protest the racist brutality of the American police state, Obama made a special point of trying to disabuse young people of the notion that direct action in the streets was superior to voting when it comes to making positive and progressive change.

The directness and intensity of Obama's rhetoric against Trump and Trumpism has been clearest and sharpest when Congressional and presidential elections are coming closer in time, as we have seen. That is no accident. It reflects Obama's electoralism—his at least outward faith in the nation's painfully time-staggered winner-take-all candidate-centered election contests as the avenue through which the citizenry gets its "input" and "democracy" is honored.

It's a foolish faith to cling to, as Obama certainly knows but would never publicly say. An abundance of social and political science data accumulated and rigorously evaluated over the years shows beyond the shadow of any serious doubt that the nation's majority progressive public opinion is close to completely irrelevant to the making of policy whereas the nation's corporate and financial ruling class generally gets what it wants from American government thanks to superior economic resources that translate naturally into dominant political power beneath and beyond the pretense of popular-self-rule.

...BUT NOT FOR ACTUAL PROGRESSIVES

All this aside (a subject tackled at length in the present author's most recent previous book *They Rule: The 1% vs. Democracy*), Obama's recurrent counsel for Americans to "VOTE" tends to beg a rather critical question: vote for who, Mr. ex-President? For Green Party and other third and fourth party candidates who run in accord with majority progressive, left-leaning public opinion by calling for universal single payer national health insurance (Medicare for All), genuinely progressive taxation, free public college, the revocation of crippling student debt, the restoration of union organizing and collective bargaining rights, substantive consumer protection, a universal basic income, massive cuts in the nation's bloated Pentagon System (which eats up more than half of federal discretionary spending and accounts for 40% of military spending the world over), and an existentially necessary Green New Deal?

Certainly not. Obama is nothing if not a major party man and his recurrently declared interest in cooperation across party lines does not extend to Left parties, who fall outside his view of "pragmatic" and "realistic" politics that can "get things done," to use one of his favorite phrases.

What about sincerely progressive Democrats like U.S. Senator and past presidential candidate Bernie Sanders and his fellow Congressional "democratic socialists" (really neo-New Deal social democrats) Alexandria Ocasio-Cortez ("AOC," D-NY), Ilhan Omar (D-MN), and Rashida Tlaib (D-MI)? Here Obama is more polite because the politicos in questions (a) have honored major party hegemony by staying within the corporate Democratic Party and (b) are highly popular with a considerable portion of the electorate that Democrats must turn out on election days to stay viable as one of the nation's two reigning political organizations. But while he might seem to respect and even perhaps somewhat admire Bernie and "the squad," Obama's status as a died-in-wool corporate Democrat in the oligarchy-climbing model of the Clintons means that he works behind the scenes with fellow corporatists across the permanent political class and "liberal" media to make sure that progressive Democrats and their "radical" policy ideas like Single Payer health insurance and free public college—policies that most Americans support—are understood as beyond the parameters of acceptable debate and realistic advocacy.

Obama therefore had nothing to say as the Hillary Clinton campaign worked hand in glove with the Democratic National Committee and the corporate media to rig the 2016 Democratic presidential campaign against Sanders. It was well understood across the establishment that his former Secretary of State, the right-wing Wall Street Democrat and "lying neoliberal warmonger" Hillary Clinton, was Obama's preferred candidate. Obama operatives were filtered across the Clinton campaign and DNC, working quietly to make sure that she defeated the "progressive populist" challenger who was running in accord with majority public policy opinion and societal values.

Obama contributed somewhat to the Democrats' victory in the 2018 mid-terms, but he clearly did so without much enthusiasm for the kind of progressive, left-leaning Democrats like AOC and her fellow "Squad" members Tlaib and the brilliant Omar. "According to several people close to him," Ryan Lizza learned in 2019, "his experience campaigning during 2018 made him even more convinced that Democrats had to be careful not to mistake the passion and excitement on Twitter for candidates like Alexandria Ocasio-Cortez for where the public was ideologically, especially in the coming general election against Trump." Obama's associates were mistaken if they thought AOC and "the Squad's" popularity was merely an Internet phenomenon, however. AOC, like Bernie Sanders, ran in accord with the nation's hidden majority progressive opinion on a broad range of political and policy issues.

None of the Squad members received open backing from Obama in the 2018 mid-term primary elections. His formal endorsement list for that year was heavily weighted towards centrist corporate Democrats in the corporate "Third Way" mode, vapidly described by Obama as "diverse, patriotic, and big-hearted."

"BARACK OBAMA WINS THE [2020] DEMOCRATIC PRIMARY"

"Voters Don't Want to See Crazy Stuff"

Obama's stance on the presidential race has been unsurprisingly positioned in the same centrist ground. Obama has been outwardly courteous and at times complimentary regarding the highly popular Bernie Sanders. Obama's language was conciliatory and even flattering towards Sanders in his formal endorsement of Biden last April:

> Now Joe will be a better candidate for having run the
> gauntlet of primaries and caucuses alongside one of the

most impressive Democratic fields ever. Each of our candidates were talented and decent with a track record of accomplishment, smart ideas and serious visions for the future, and that is certainly true of the candidate who made it farther than any other, Bernie Sanders. Bernie is an American original, a man who has devoted his life to giving voice to working people's hopes, dreams and frustrations. He and I haven't always agreed on everything, but we have always shared a conviction that we have to make America a fairer, more just, more equitable society. We both know that nothing is more powerful than millions of voices calling for change, and the ideas he has championed, the energy and enthusiasm he inspired, especially in young people, will be critical in moving America in a direction of progress and hope because for the second time in 12 years we will have the incredible task of rebuilding our economy, and to meet the moment, the Democratic Party will have to be bold.

This chummy rhetoric hid some nasty history. We can be sure that the insidious corporate centrism of most of the 2019–20 Democratic presidential candidate field—well to the right of actual majority-progressive public opinion on key policy issues and values—bore the imprint of Obama's centrist example and counsel. By Lizza's account, "Every Democratic presidential campaign starts with what one close adviser to Barack Obama calls 'The Pilgrimage'"—a journey to Obama's office in the West End of Washington D.C. The content of the tutorials and advice Obama gave to Warren, Sanders, Buttigieg, Kamala Harris, Cory Booker, Beto O'Rourke, Steve Bullock and others are private. We can be sure that Obama warned all the candidates other than Sanders and perhaps Warren to stay away from the "radical" (mildly social-democratic) Sanders and AOC tendency. The incessant sniping that Sanders and Warren received on the primary debate stages over the supposed radical extremism and unaffordability of their highly affordable and moderately progressive policy proposals (Single Payer health insurance, free public college, and green jobs) came straight out of the corporate-ideological "neoliberal" Clinton-Obama playbook. It was Obama's close ally and former White House chief of staff Rahm Emanuel who got the ball rolling with the absurd and vicious 2019 and 2020 charge that Sanders' struggle to advance health care as a human right was actually an attempt to throw millions of American off of health insurance—a charge that would be repeated by the Obamaist-Clintonite candidates Buttigieg, Booker, O'Rourke, and Klobuchar during the primary campaign.

In Lizza's in-depth November 2019 account, there was one exception to Obama's avowed determination not to intervene in the presidential primary for or against a candidate: Bernie Sanders. "Back when Sanders seemed like more of a threat than he does now," Lizza learned, "Obama said privately that if Bernie were running away with the nomination, Obama would speak up to stop him."[1] Lizza failed to note that Obama's threat was far from private—it was certainly leaked with a purpose. Moreover, Lizza did not seem to appreciate what a remarkable and transparently corporatist step it would have been for the nation's previous president to have intervened publicly against Sanders, thereby undermining Sanders' future viability against Trump, had Sanders started to sweep the Democratic nomination. The threat to intervene "if Bernie were running away" was *no small matter*.

"Obama mostly stuck to his pledge not to interfere in the [presidential] race," Lizza learned in the spring of 2020, "but in 2019 there was an enormously important exception. In mid-November at a democratic donor event he weighed in forcefully on the left vs. centrist argument that was then dominating the race. He warned Democratic candidates not to confuse actual voters with 'left-leaning Twitter feeds.' He said that that voters 'don't want to see crazy stuff, that America is 'less revolutionary that it is interested in improvement'...."[2] As the *New York Times* elaborated last April, Obama "offered thinly veiled criticism of Mr. Sanders' 'revolutionary policies and opined that voters wanted change, not to 'tear down the system.'"[3] In this "warning about the electoral consequences of leftism," as Lizza called it, Obama channeled the standard corporate smear absurdly claiming that the basic progressive programs supported by most Americans and championed by Sanders and his many backers—Medicare for All, progressive taxation, consumer protection, the Green New Deal and more—were "crazy," excessively radical ("revolutionary") efforts to "tear down the system," and contrary to ordinary Americans' hope for a bettering of their conditions. It was a revolting display of Obama's deeply conservative world view.

"A DELICATE TASK"

When the "democratic socialist" Sanders surged and did in fact threaten to "run away with the nomination" by winning the Iowa Caucus popular vote and the New Hampshire and Nevada primaries in February of 2020, Obama did in fact intervene against the progressive Senator from Vermont. He did so behind the scenes, encouraging his fellow corporate and Wall Street Democrats Pete Buttigieg and Amy Klobuchar to call off their campaigns so that "moderates" (corporatists) could unite behind the right-wing corporate Democrat Joe Biden to finish off Sanders in the primary race.

"Obama," Lizza found in April 2020, "had a delicate task. Everyone knew who he preferred"—Joe Biden—but "he could not be seen as helping organize the massive party-wide show of force in favor of Biden that emerged from South Carolina through Super Tuesday. Obama's aides forcefully reiterated that he was scrupulously not intervening."

The claim of non-intervention was a lie. "But some of his aides," Lizza learned, "now concede that behind the scenes Obama played a role in nudging things in Biden's direction at the crucial movement when the Biden team was organizing former candidates to coalesce around Biden. 'I know he did a few things,' said one longtime closer adviser to Obama. He was talking to Biden regularly in that period. I don't know exactly what he said, but you can speculate. It's noteworthy that he called Klobuchar and others right when they got out." The *Times* reported that Obama told Buttigieg that "he'd never have more leverage than on the day he quit the race" and "joined the avalanche of former candidates backing Mr. Biden."[4]

In an April 14th *New York Times* report on "Obama's Role in Wrapping Up the Primary," the paper's Obama beat writer Glenn Thrush observed that Obama's claim of neutrality in the Sanders-Biden contest was less than completely truthful. "With calibrated stealth," Thrush learned from Obama insiders, "Mr. Obama has been more engaged in the campaign's denouement than previously revealed even before he endorsed Biden today. For months, Mr. Obama had kept in contact with senior party officials, in hopes of preventing a repeat of the protracted and nasty 2016 primary race."

Among other things, Thrush learned that Obama had played an important role in convincing Sanders to surrender early in the primary contest. In late March, Thrush reported, Obama spoke two or three times to Sanders, "reassuring [him] that he had already accomplished much of what he had set out to do, moving the party—and Mr. Biden—substantially to the left." It was time, Obama told a friend, to "accelerate the endgame." And it was effective, according to Sanders insiders who told Thrush that "Obama's effort to ease the senator out of the race played a significant role in Mr. Sanders' decision to end his bid and endorse Mr. Biden."

Along the way, Obama communicated his approval of the Biden campaign's February decision to make Jennifer O'Malley, a former Obama campaign official, Biden's campaign manager, and to place another top Obama veteran, Anita Dunn, into a powerful position.

Perhaps someday we will learn that Obama and/or his team played a role in convincing the sometime semi-progressive

Elizabeth Warren not to throw her support to Sanders in the wake of her defeat.

"Obama was very careful not to be seen as putting a thumb on the scale," an Obama insider who knew about Obama's call to Buttigieg told Lizza last April. "He and the people close to him are very careful about the optics—the 2016-style optics. Sanders and his supporters have reason to believe the party put the thumb on the scale for Hillary in 2016 and he wanted to avoid that. Obama…was very cautious and discreet in how he operated."

Translation: *Obama used his considerable influence to help install the stumbling right-wing corporate Democrat Joe Biden (see below) as the nominee to take on the "the most dangerous criminal in human history" but Obama was careful not to be seen as doing what he did.*

Lizza's report bore a chillingly accurate title: "*Barack Obama Wins the Democratic Primary.*"

"YOU KNOW THE THING": CORPORATE LY'N IMPERIAL AND RACIST JOE

Here it is worth recalling that the blunderer Biden wouldn't be on the national political stage in 2020 but for Obama's decision to choose the twice-failed presidential candidate to be his running mate in 2008. The decision was made largely out of the calculation that Biden would "help Obama win over older voters worried he was too young and too inexperienced."

Now, "Obamaworld"—Lizza's phrase for the big team of Obama administration alumni and current Obama staff—"believe[d]—perhaps naively—that the former president will have a role in helping Biden with younger voters."

Good luck! Obama's 77 year-old 2020 candidate is the *absolute opposite of bold and progressive.* Is Joe Biden suffering from dementia, as many observers familiar with aging and cognitive decline contend? Such an assessment is beyond the professional purview of the present writer. Biden has exhibited behaviors consistent with the diagnosis: confusing New Hampshire with Vermont during a campaign stop; not knowing the name of the college where he just spoke; incorrectly thinking that he met with Parkland school shooting victims when he was vice president; invading the centrist MSDNC host Joy Reid's physical space to claim that she advocated "physical revolution;" serial incidents of inappropriate public touching (and sniffing); confusing his wife with his sister on stage; forgetting thoughts in mid-sentence; saying that the Dayton and El Paso mass shootings took place in "Michigan" and "Houston;" telling a bizarre and meandering story about a supposed adolescent confrontation with a Black tough named "Corn Pop" outside a segregated swimming pool; calling an Iowa voter "fat" and "too old to vote for me;" claiming that he would have "beat up Trump in high school;" calling a young woman voter in New Hampshire "a dog-faced pony soldier."

Celebrating a big primary victory in Texas this March, Biden briefly turned Super Tuesday into "Super Thursday" before horribly mangling the Declaration of Independence. "We hold these truths to be self-evident," he started off and then collapsed into "All men and women created by...go...you know...*you know the thing*!"

For some politicians, and Biden appears to be one of them, age is a relevant voter concern. Obama is quite aware of this, which may be part of why he waited to endorse Biden in the presidential primary until it was clear that none of the former vice president's considerably younger and more articulate moderate challengers (especially Kamala Harris) would seize the nomination. "When a Democratic donor raised the issue of Mr. Biden's age late last year," the *New York Times* reported this June, "Obama acknowledged those concerns, saying 'I wasn't even 50 when I got elected, and that job took every ounce of energy I had.'"

LY'N JOE

While all this raises the troubling question of executive function in the brain of a potential future chief executive, a bigger problem is that Biden has showed unmistakable signs of power- and self-serving moral decrepitude across his long and unimpressive, corporate-Democratic and imperial career. During his dismally unsuccessful campaign for the 1988 Democratic presidential nomination, Biden stole key lines and themes from the British Labor Party candidate Neil Kinnock, falsely portraying himself as a working-class hero who rose up from generations of coal miners. After it came out that Biden had ripped off the English politician, Biden gave a speech crediting Kinnock but claiming that he'd received a videotape of the Kinnock speech he plagiarized from "a leader of another country." In reality, Biden got the speech from a Washington political consultant who had made the tape available to numerous candidates.

Joe's oratorical pilfering of Kinnock was not plagiarism technically speaking since political speeches don't bear copyrights. During law school, however, Biden committed plagiarism the real thing. He took five pages from a law review article for a brief he wrote in a legal methodology course. Biden was penalized with an 'F' for the course, which he had to repeat.

Another example of morally problematic deception concerns the tragic death of his young wife and infant daughter in a traffic accident in December of 1972. In September of 2001, one week after the 9/11 jetliner attacks, Biden told nearly three thousand people at the University of Delaware that his wife and daughter had been killed by "an errant driver who stopped to drink instead of drive."

Six years later, while running for president again in Iowa, he told an Iowa City audience that the driver of the truck that hit his wife and daughter "allegedly drank his lunch instead of eating his lunch." This was simply false. As *POLITICO*'s Michael Kruse reported last January:

The problem was it wasn't true. The driver of the truck, Curtis C. Dunn of Pennsylvania, was not charged with drunk driving. He wasn't charged with anything. The accident was an accident, and though the police file no longer exists, coverage in the newspapers at the time made it clear that fault was not in question. For whatever reason, Neilia Biden, who was holding the baby, ended up in the right of way of Dunn's truck coming down a long hill.

"She had a stop sign. The truck driver did not," Jerome Herlihy told me. He's a retired judge who then was a deputy attorney general and once was a neighbor to Biden and remains friendly. A pal of Biden at the time asked Herlihy "to go out to the state police troop where the driver of the other vehicle was to make sure everything was going all right," and so he did. "In the end," Herlihy said, "I concurred in their decision that there was no fault on his part."

Biden's lie, centered on the deaths of his first wife and baby daughter, upset the family of Curtis Dunn, who died in 1999. Dunn had lived his last twenty-seven years with the painful memory of what happened when Biden's first wife recklessly pulled out in front of him with her baby in her lap.

What led Biden to falsely attribute the tragedy to a drunk driver? Kruse bends over backwards to provide psychological rationalizations (he speculates that Biden used the lie to make the deaths "more palatable" and that Biden just likes to stretch the truth) but the 2007 version of the lie, uttered in the context of his Iowa presidential campaign, surely reflected a desire to curry sympathy points from voters. It's not a pretty picture.

Consistent with concerns that Biden bends the truth for political advantage, the *Washington Post* outed him for concocting a ridiculous tale about his heroic role in honoring a medal-winning U.S. soldier in a war zone as vice president. It was no small fib. By the *Post*'s account, "Biden got the time period, the location, the heroic act, the military branch, and the rank of the recipient wrong as well as his own role in the ceremony."

Biden tried to win Black primary votes in South Carolina this year by falsely claiming to have been arrested while trying to visit Nelson Mandela in jail during the apartheid era in South Africa. This was a bald-faced lie.

Last January, during a debate, Biden claimed that he argued against George W. Bush's monumentally criminal and mass-murderous invasion of Iraq immediately after it began. In fact, it took Biden two years to admit that Bush's war and Biden's own Senate vote to authorize it were "mistakes" (try 'crimes').

IMPERIAL JOE

Biden, it is worth recalling, didn't merely go along with the march to illegal imperial war on Mesopotamia. He led the charge from the Democratic side of the U.S. Senate. This is consistent with a long imperialist Biden record that includes enthusiastic support for gigantic Pentagon budgets, the Carter and Reagan administration's sponsorship of Islamic terrorism in Afghanistan, Ronald Reagan's Central American proxy wars, George H.W. Bush's Persian Gulf War, Bush senior and Bill Clinton's mass murderous economic sanctions on Iraq, George W. Bush's criminal invasion of Afghanistan, Barack Obama's record-setting drone wars, Obama and Hillary Clinton's support for a right-wing coup in Honduras, Obama's destruction of Libya, and Obama's sponsorship of a right-wing coup in Ukraine. Consistent with this imperial war-mongering record, Biden this summer criticized Trump for failing to follow through on threats to overthrow the democratically elected socialist government of Venezuela. Biden is naturally a militant backer of the apartheid and occupation state of Israel and its relentless torture of the Palestinian people.

Not that he plays at being an anti-imperialist. That is one bit of progressive pretense he does not indulge in beyond lying to cover up his leading support for so-called Operation Iraqi Liberation.

CORPORATE WALL STREET JOE

Biden's worst deception may be his pretense of being "lunch-bucket Joe," a product and friend of the working-class. His fiercely corporatist and pro-Wall Street record militates against this blue-collar branding:

- Voting to rollback bankruptcy protections for college graduates (1978) and vocational school graduates (1984) with federal student loans.

- Working with Republican allies to pass the Bankruptcy Abuse Prevention and Consumer Protection Act, which put traditional "clean slate" Chapter 7 bankruptcy out of reach for millions of ordinary Americans and thousands of small businesses (2005).

- Voting against a bill that would have compelled credit card companies to warn customers of the costs of only making minimum payments.

- Honoring campaign donations from Coca-Cola by co-sponsoring a bill that permitted soft-drink producers to skirt antitrust laws (1979).

- Joining just one other Congressional Democrat to vote against a Judiciary Committee measure to increase consumers' rights to sue corporations for price-fixing (1979).

- Strongly supporting the 1999 Gramm–Leach–Bliley Act, which permitted the re-merging of investment and commercial banking by repealing the Depression-era Glass–Steagall Act. (This helped create the 2007–8 financial crisis and subsequent recession.)

- Supporting the corporate-neoliberal North American Free Trade agreement and the globalist investor rights Trans-Pacific Partnership.

Adding plutocratic insult to oligarchic policy injury, candidate Biden has criticized those who advocate a universal basic income—the necessity of which has been highlighted by the mass unemployment of the new Great Depression sparked by the COVID-19 crisis—of "selling American workers short" and undermining the "dignity" of work. He opposes calls for free college tuition, Single Payer health insurance, and large-scale green jobs programs as "too radical" and "too expensive." He defends Big Business from popular criticism, writing in 2017 that "Some want to single out big corporations for all the blame. … But consumers, workers, and leaders have the power to hold every corporation to a higher standard, not simply cast business as the enemy." That's called propagating a fantasy—the existence of a democratic political system in which the working-class majority has the power to hold concentrated wealth accountable.

"I don't think five hundred billionaires are the reason we're in trouble. The folks at the top aren't bad guys," Biden sickeningly told the Brookings Institution last year—this as he claimed to worry about how the "gap is yawning" between the American super-rich and everyone else.

Most nauseating of all, "blue-collar" Biden said that he has "no empathy" for Millennials' struggle to get by in the savagely unequal and insecure precariat economy he helped create over his many years of abject service to the Lords of Capital. "The younger generation now tells me how tough things are—give me a break," said Biden, while speaking to Patt Morrison of *the Los Angeles Times* last year. "No, no, I have no empathy for it, give me a break."

"No, no, I have no empathy for it, give me a break." So what if Millennials face a significant diminution of opportunity, wealth, income and security compared to the Baby Boomers with whom Biden identifies? Who cares if "lunch bucket Joe" helped shrink the American Dream for young people with the neoliberal policies and politics he helped advance?

Biden's low standing with young Americans during the primary race was richly deserved, to say the least.

Consistent with his longstanding crass corporatism and ruling class elitism, Biden suggested in early March that he would veto Medicare for All—single payer health insurance as a human right if it came to his desk as president. The timing of his right-wing suggestion could not have been worse: it came just as the COVID-19 crisis began to sweep the nation, leading to the removal of millions of Americans from their jobs and therefore from health insurance thanks to America's long-outdated system of largely employment-based health insurance.

Biden has naturally offered no substantive criticism of the giant bipartisan corporate bailout that the Trump administration and Congress created in response the COVID-19 recession. The "rescue" package funnels hundreds of billions of taxpayer dollars to the wealthy Few's giant corporations and financial institutions and a comparative pittance to the nation's working class majority while Americans have been thrown out of work at a record-setting pace. It contains no caps on corporate CEO's outrageous salaries or the returns on elite investment.

"NOTHING WOULD FUNDAMENTALLY CHANGE"

Nobody who has paid serious attention to Biden's 2020 campaign should be surprised. Speaking to rich donors at a ritzy New York fundraiser in June of 2019, Biden promised his listeners that "nothing would fundamentally change" if he is elected. Biden obediently told top Manhattan financial and election investors that he would not "demonize" the rich and promised that "no one's standard of living will change, nothing would fundamentally change"—a revealing promise made shortly after he had made a bizarre and off-putting appearance at the Poor People's Campaign Presidential Forum in Washington. Biden said that excessive poverty was "the one thing that can bring this country down" but added that "We have all the money we need to" fix the problem. No big tax raises on the rich and no essential change in policy and world views would be required: "I mean, we may not want to demonize anybody who has made money.... The truth of the matter is, you all, you all know, you all know in your gut what has to be done. We can disagree in the margins but the truth of the matter is it's all within our wheelhouse and nobody has to be punished. No one's standard of living will change, nothing would fundamentally change."

Biden went on to say that the rich should not be blamed for income inequality, pleading to the donors, "I need you very badly."

"I hope if I win this nomination, I won't let you down. I promise you," he added.

It was a moment of pure slavish devotion to the corporate and financial bourgeoisie.

"NEVER CALLED ME BOY"

Sadly and ironically enough, Biden was the preferred candidate of older Black voters during the 2020 presidential primaries. That position, fed to no small extent by his eight ears as number two to the nation's first technically Black president, was richly undeserved. Proud of his onetime alliance with openly segregationist, racially terrorist Jim Crow U.S. Senators like James O. Eastland—the one who Biden (forgetting his own skin color?) said "never called me 'boy'" in June of 2019—Biden backed the racist mass incarceration state by supporting Bill Clinton's 1994 'Three Strikes" crime and prison bill along with Clinton and Newt Gingrich's vicious abolition of Aid for Families with Dependent Children. Biden took his embrace of the supposedly sacred virtue of bipartisanship to the grotesque level of forming close friendships with virulent southern white racists like Republican Senators Strom Thurmond and Jesse Helms (not to mention the frothing warmonger John McCain—a natural ally given Biden's longstanding imperialism). Biden responded to a debate question about racial inequality, segregation, and the legacy of slavery last September by *smirking and then strangely telling Black parents to "put on the television, I mean the record player"* to help educate their children.

In a June 2020 letter warning Biden that he might lose to Trump if he failed to back more progressive policing policies in the wake of the George Floyd rebellion, fifty national liberal and progressive organizations offered scathing commentary on Biden's racially troubling criminal justice record:

> In the course of your political career, you have designed and endorsed policies that have significantly exacerbated [racial oppression]…As a Senator, you not only supported, but in many cases authored and championed laws that expanded mass incarceration, increased police powers, and exacerbated racial disparities in surveillance and sentencing. These laws … are a part of the history that has led us to this moment, and their ongoing fallout has contributed to the outpourings of grief and anger we are seeing today…You have a moral responsibility in this moment [to atone for past policies you supported that] broke apart Black communities and robbed many young Black people of a future.

(During the Democratic presidential primary debates, even the centrist and white-pleasing Obama-style Senator Cory Booker [D-NJ] was moved to accurately describe Biden as an "architect of mass incarceration").

The activists and groups who signed this letter were unimpressed by Biden's "comprehensive plan" to overhaul the nation's racially disparate policing and sentencing laws:

> Making amends for the harm you've caused is an important first step, but it is no longer enough….you've taken some positive positions—including calling for a federal ban on police chokeholds—but these too are far from sufficient. In order to rise to this occasion, you must put forward a transformative and comprehensive policing and criminal justice platform that shifts how we approach public safety and allows Black communities in particular to thrive.

The groups demanded that Biden drop his proposal to add $300 million in funding for the Community Oriented Policing Services (COPS) program, which would hire and train additional police officers to patrol inner-city communities. It was an offensive and ill-time proposal to put forward while tens of millions took to the streets, facing tear gas in at least 100 cities and towns, to protest racist police brutality in the wake of the George Floyd and Brionna Taylor murders and a public health emergency that was inflicting special misery on the Black community. As masses chanted "Defund the Police," advocating serious proposals to shift public resources from social repression to social uplift and protection when it came to the plight of Black communities, Biden called for increased funding to local militarized and racist police! And this while going on a Black political talk show to tell a popular Black radio personality that "you ain't Black" if you weren't going to vote for Biden.

As if this wasn't insulting enough to Black voters, Biden in mid-July ludicrously described Trump as the nation's "first racist president"—an openly absurd statement in a nation whose top position had been held by numerous slave-owners between 1789 and 1860 and by openly racist segregationists like Woodrow Wilson in subsequent years.

Meanwhile, Biden has had nothing to say in defense of Black voting rights, which are under harsh and potentially decisive attack in 2020 as in past elections. "The purges from the rolls, closed polling places and other methods of disenfranchisement are continuing," writes Margaret Kimberly, "without comment from the Democrats who ignore their most loyal and important cohort."[5]

In this and countless other ways, Joe Biden is a great insult to the nation's citizens and the democratic ideal.

SO WHAT?

With Sanders comfortably swept into the dustbin of American political history with the "behind the scenes" help of Obama last April, Obama was "free[d] up…to live up to what he said—that he wasn't going to put his thumb on the scale until there was a nominee." So said a "longtime Obama adviser" (almost certainly David Axlerod) to Ryan Lizza last spring, with no apparent shame for the Orwellian absurdity of his comment. "Now," the Obama adviser added, "he'll do anything the party and nominee want to help win the election."

So what if Sanders was the Democratic presidential candidate most likely to organize the majority of working-class Americans who the corporate Democrats—the nation's Inauthentic Opposition Party of Fake Resistance (IOPFR)—have been betraying and demobilizing for decades? So what if this made Sanders the most electable candidate against an incumbent president and a party that pose grave fascistic and eco-cidal threats to what's left of democracy, the republic, and life itself? So what if Sanders' key policy proposals, including Single Payer health insurance (health care as a human right) and a Green New Deal (to put millions to work trying to roll back the capitalist destruction of livable ecology) are urgently required for the common good and human survival? So what if Sanders' proposals are conservative in relation to the savage scale of the inequality and environmental destruction neoliberal class rule has been inflicting for several decades on Americans and livable ecology? And so what if nearly half (47%) of Sanders supporters would not commit to voting for the Democratic presidential candidate in November if it wasn't Bernie?

The Democratic establishment was determined to stop Sanders at all costs and in numerous ways.[6] As the present author has been arguing for years, one of the corporate Democrats' dirty little secrets is that they would rather lose to the ever more viciously right-wing Republicans and the demented fascist oligarch

Trump than to the moderately left wing of their own party. The Democratic Party isn't about social justice, democracy, and/or environmental sanity. It isn't even primarily about winning elections. "History's second most enthusiastic capitalist party" (as former Nixon strategist Kevin Phillips once accurately described the Democrats) is about serving "elite" corporate and financial sponsors above all, and those sponsors preferred a second fascistic Trump term to a mildly progressive first Sanders one. As an agent of the corporate Democratic Party establishment, Obama has used his status and power to keep the party's big bankrollers happy by making sure that Joe Biden was the Democrats' contender against "the most dangerous criminal in human history."

"THE ESSENCE OF AMERICAN POLITICS"

In late July of 2020, as the present book neared its completion deadline, Biden released a campaign commercial aired across the pivotal battleground state of Ohio. It was a state-of-the-art production. Portraying Biden as a sturdy son of the proletariat in Scranton, Pennsylvania, the campaign identified Biden with "the backbone of the nation—working families," engaged in an epic peoples' struggle with "those at the top": the rich and powerful, represented by Donald Trump. "This crisis," Biden's slick and emotionally potent commercial said, "has revealed that we must do more for workers and small businesses, not the wealthy." Biden's clever, well-crafted slogan was "Build Back Better."

Sadly, the commercial had nothing whatsoever to do with Biden's richly corporatist and imperial record (related above) as a U.S. Senator and Vice President. That record shows consistent service precisely to "those at the top," the wealthy Few, and suggests that a Biden presidency will follow in the footsteps of the Clinton and Obama presidencies by being loaded with friends and representatives of the nation's financial and corporate wealth and power elite.

The commercial epitomized what a still leftish Christopher Hitchens once called (in a brilliant and bitter book on the Clintons) "the essence of American politics": "the manipulation of populism by elitism."

"I'd vote for anybody over Trump," the angry writer Drew Magary asked last April, "but did it have to be THIS anybody? Thanks to Obama, I guess it does."

Once again: *Thanks, Obama!*

POSTSCRIPT (AUGUST 13, 2020)

After this chapter was completed, Obama released a list of Congressional and state-level candidates that he was endorsing in the upcoming 2020 elections. Progressive Democrats running on behalf of majority-backed calls for Single Payer national health insurance, free public college, and a Green New Deal were noticeably absent from his centrist roster. Not a single "Squad" member made the list.

Adding more insult to Black voters, Biden told an online convention of Black and Latinx journalists that the Black community lacked "diversity" when compared to the Latinx community—a remark for which he had to quickly apologize.

It is safe to assume that Obama was consulted on the selection of the conservative corporate Democrat and U.S. Senator Kamala Harris as Biden's running mate. Obama has long been a fan of Senator Harris, who is in many ways a female version of Obama. As a presidential candidate and president, Obama's commitment to the defense of existing socioeconomic, racial, and imperial power and oppression structures was cloaked to no small degree by his technically Black identity. Like the former president, Harris's deeply conservative record (including a history of sending large numbers of Black and Latinx offenders to prison with a tough "law and order" approach as a California prosecutor and Attorney General) is cloaked by deceptive, progressive-sounding rhetoric and imagery and by her technically non-white status. Being female gives her further identity-politics credit with liberal elites.

Adding more insult to progressive Democrats in the Sanders mode, the charismatic AOC was granted a paltry 60 seconds of speaking time at the upcoming online Democratic National Convention. Obama will of course be the main featured speaker at this event. He will face no such draconian time limits as he gives what can be expected to be his most forceful critique of Trump to date—a trend that will continue up through the election given Obama's pattern of strictly calibrating the volume and intensity of his rhetoric to the constitutionally mandated election cycle. It will be interesting to see if Obama actually mentions Trump by name.

ENDNOTES

1. Lizza, "Waiting for Obama."

2. Ryan Lizza, "Barack Obama Wins the Democratic Primary," *POLITICO*, April 9, 2020.

3. Glenn Thrush, "Accelerate the Endgame: Obama's Role in Wrapping Up the Primary," *New York Times*, April 14, 2020.

4. Thrush, "Accelerate the Endgame."

5. Margaret Kimberley, "Freedom Rider: Democrats Move Right and to Defeat," *Monthly Review*, June 25, 2020, https://mronline.org/2020/06/25/freedom-rider-democrats-move-right-and-towards-defeat/?fbclid=IwAR0G-doUqkU8fScrcnDRG5vHzECsy5AAK27ACVimqB6HW5i8b_l-DOwEZaqs

6. Paul Street, "The Game is Rigged," *CounterPunch*, February 7, 2020, https://www.counterpunch.org/2020/02/07/the-game-is-rigged/

CHAPTER SIX

Obama Being Obama: A Hollow Man Filled With Ruling Class Ideas

> In his view of history, in his respect for tradition, in his skepticism that the world can be changed any way but very, very slowly, *Obama is deeply conservative*...It's not just that he thinks revolutions are unlikely: he *values continuity and stability for their own sake, sometimes even more than he values change for the good.* [Emphasis added]
> —Larissa MacFarquhar, May 7, 2007

Nobody who knows the forty-fourth president's real history should be surprised by his tepid response to the disastrous Trump administration. On the last page of his monumental, incredibly detailed, 1078-page biography *Rising Star: The Making of Barack Obama*, the Pulitzer Prize-winning historian David J. Garrow describes Obama at the end of his "failed presidency" as a man who had long ago become a "vessel [that] was hollow at its core." It's a stunningly personal and negative judgement.

As was the case in Garrow's classic 1986 biography of Dr. Martin Luther King, Jr.[1], *Rising Star*, published in 2017, gets personal. Garrow notes how disappointed and betrayed many of Obama's former friends felt by a president who "doesn't feel indebted to people" (in the words of a former close assistant) and who spent inordinate presidential down time on the golf course and "celebrity hobnobbing." Garrow quotes one of Obama's "long-time Hyde Park [Chicago] friend[s]," who offered a stark judgement: "Barack is a tragic figure: so much potential, such critical times, but such a failure to perform...like he is an empty shell...Maybe the flaw is hubris, deep and abiding hubris...."

Garrow reports, too, the complaints of Obama's three former girlfriends, Alex McNair, Genevieve Cook, and Sheila Jager. Each one recalls Obama as maddeningly inaccessible and self-involved.

Ms. Jager was a University of Chicago anthropology graduate student when she met Obama. Her experiences garner special attention from Garrow. During the late 1980s, Jager fell into a prolonged and ardent affair with Obama, who was at the time a community organizer. Her long, tumultuous relationship with the future president was doomed by the color of her skin: Jager was of Dutch and Japanese ancestry. Obama shared her passion but decided he could not marry because his political ambitions, both in Chicago and beyond, required a Black spouse. As a young woman, Jager, now an Oberlin College anthropology professor, was frustrated by young Obama's lack of "courage." Writing to Garrow in August of 2013, Jager reflected on the spinelessness of Obama's excessively "pragmatic," disengaged, and "compromising" presidency:

> The seeds of his future failings were always present in Chicago. He made a series of calculated decisions when he began to map out his political life at the time and they involved some deep compromises. There is a familiar echo in the language he uses now to talk about the compromises he's always forced to make and the way he explained his future to me back then, saying in effect I "wish" I could do this, but "pragmatism and the reality of the world has forced me to do that." From the bailout out to NSA to Egypt, it is always the same. The problem is that "pragmatism" can very much look like what works best for the moment. Hence, the constant criticism that there is no strategic vision behind his decisions. Perhaps this pragmatism and need to just "get along in the world" (by accepting the world as it is instead of trying to change it) stems from his deep-seated need to be loved and admired which has ultimately led him on the path to conformism and not down the path of greatness which I had hoped for him.

Garrow's mammoth biography is a *tour de force* of detailed historical inquiry and psychological critique. His mastery of the smallest details in Obama's life and career and his ability to place those facts within a narrative that keeps the reader's attention (no small feat at 1078 pages!) is remarkable. *Rising Star* falls short, however, on ideological appraisal. In early 1996, the brilliant Black leftist Adolph Reed, Jr., a political scientist, captured the vapid moral and political limits of what would become the Obama phenomenon, forecasting the gist of Obama's work at the state level, nationally, and finally throughout the Weimar-like Barack Von Obombdenburg presidency. Reflecting on an unnamed Obama in the *Village Voice*, Reed wrote this memorable paragraph:

> In Chicago…we've gotten a foretaste of the new breed of foundation-hatched black communitarian voices; one of them, a smooth Harvard lawyer with impeccable do-good credentials and vacuous-to-repressive neoliberal politics, has won a state senate seat on a base mainly in the liberal foundation and development worlds. His fundamentally *bootstrap* line was softened by a patina of the rhetoric of authentic community, talk about meeting in kitchens, small-scale solutions to social problems, and the predictable elevation of process over program—the point where identity politics converges with old-fashioned middle-class reform in favoring form over substance.

Garrow only partially quotes Reed's reflection and then disparages his insights by inaccurately dismissing them as "an academic's way of calling Barack an Uncle Tom." That is an unfortunate judgement. Reed's assessment was richly born-out by Obama's subsequent political career. Hardly anyone remembers Obama's telling centrist years in the Illinois Senate, where the future president became a darling of corporate campaign contributors and lobbyists while working closely with Republican lawmakers to shelve and water down progressive legislation (this history is detailed in the first chapter, titled "Obama's 'Dollar Value,'" of my 2008 book *Barack Obama and the Future of American Politics*).

Obama continued in the same fake-progressive, bipartisan, centrist vein during his four years in the U.S. Senate and then in the White House. Like his ideological soul-brothers Bill Clinton and Tony Blair (and perhaps now Emmanuel Macron), Obama's public life has been a wretched monument to the dark grip of ruling class corporate ideology, values, and agendas—financial and imperial agendas that lurk behind telegenic, silver-tongued, and faux-progressive façades.

Reed's prescient verdict brings considerable clarity to the tragedy that is Obama. The tragedy began unfolding before his presidency and gained steam during his two terms as the nation's chief executive. It continues now after his presidency. Obama's cringing attachment to supposedly (and deceptively) non-ideological perspectives, characterized by favorite slogans such as "get things done" "pragmatism," "compromise," and "playing it safe," or as Jager put it, "accepting the world as it is instead of trying to change it," was not merely a personality quirk or psychological flaw. Rather, this was (and remains) a longstanding strategy for outwardly "liberal" (but in reality corporative-captive) Democrats to appear "tough-minded" and stoutly determined to "get things done." Obama's "pragmatism," supposedly a concern for policy effectiveness, basically became a way to institute little change, and to govern in accord with the wishes of the nation's ruling class. This was, of course, no totally new story—"liberal" presidents have long enjoyed the wealth- and power-serving leeway that such "pragmatism" affords them.

Garrow might also have consulted a now largely forgotten New Left political science classic, Bruce Miroff's *Pragmatic Illusions: The Presidential Politics of John F. Kennedy* (1976). After detailing the supposedly progressive Kennedy's cool-headed, Harvard-minted, and "best and brightest" service to the nation's reigning corporate, imperial, and racial hierarchies, Miroff explained that:

> Most modern presidents have claimed the title of "pragmatist" for themselves. Richard Nixon was just as concerned as John Kennedy and Lyndon Johnson to announce that he was not wedded to dogma, and that his administration would follow a realistic and flexible course. It has chiefly

been the liberal presidents, however, who have captured the pragmatic label...

...For liberal presidents—and for those who have advised them—the essential mark of pragmatism is its "tough-mindedness." Pragmatism is equated with the intellectual and moral strength that can accept a world stripped of illusions and can take the facts unadorned. Committed to liberal objectives, yet free from liberal sentimentality, the pragmatic liberal sees himself as grappling with brute and unpleasant facts of political reality in order to humanize and soften those facts...

The great enemy for pragmatic liberals is "ideology"... An illusory objectivity is one of the pillars of pragmatic 'tough-mindedness.' The second pillar is readiness for power. Pragmatists are interested in what works; their prime criterion of value is success...[and] as a believer in concrete results, the pragmatist is ineluctably drawn to power. For it is power that gets things done most easily, that makes things work most successfully.

The master corporate Democrat Bill Clinton embraced the pragmatic and non-ideological "get things done" façade to promote cold-blooded capitalist and imperialist policy. So did the pivotal post-New Deal corporate Democrat Jimmy Carter and the great corporate liberals Franklin D. Roosevelt, John F. Kennedy, and Lyndon B. Johnson. Was this because they were psychologically wounded, desperate to be loved and admired in the ways suggested by professors Jager and Garrow regarding Obama? The deeper and more relevant reality is that they, like President Obama, functioned atop a nation-state ruled by unelected and interrelated dictatorships of money, empire, and white supremacism. They were educated, socialized, and indoctrinated to understand in their bones that those *de facto* dictatorships must remain intact (Roosevelt boasted of having "saved" the amoral profits system) and that liberal "reform" must always accommodate the reigning institutions and doctrines of concentrated wealth, class, race, and power. Some or all of them may well have believed and internalized the purportedly non-ideological ideology of wealth-and power-serving "pragmatism."

Obama became a true believer early on, or at least someone who cynically chose to impersonate a "true believer," in order to fast-track his rise to power. *Rising Star* shows that Obama was fully formed as a fake-progressive and neoliberal corporate Democrat well before he ever received his first campaign contribution from a Chicago area capitalist. In fact, he was headed down the same ideological path as the Clintons before Bill Clinton even walked into the Oval Office. Obama's years in the corporate-funded foundation world, the ruling and professional class finishing schools Columbia University and Harvard Law, and the standard-bearing neoliberal University of Chicago Law School minted him as a sharp if "vacuous to repressive neoliberal" by the early and middle 1990s. During his years at Harvard Law, Garrow notes, Obama gave a hint of his future strategy during a Turner Broadcasting African American Summit in the 1990s:

> Whenever we blame society for everything, or blame white racism for everything, then inevitably we're giving away our own power…if we can get start getting beyond some of these old divisions [of race, place, and class] and look at the possibilities of crafting pragmatic, practical strategies that are going to focus on what's going to make it work and less about whether it fits into one ideological mold or another.

These were classic ruling and professional class narratives at the height of the post-New Deal, post-Cold War neoliberal era.

Along with a healthy dose of market economics, this was the deceptively "non-ideological" essence of much of Obama's work at Harvard Law, where he and his good friend, the former economist Rob Fisher, were drawn to the courses of a libertarian professor and wrote about the supposed progressive and democratic potential of "market forces." Like other elite institutions of higher education, Harvard Law was and remains a great schoolhouse of precisely the kind of "pragmatism" which insisted that no policy, social, or political vision could work if it didn't bow to the holy power of the corporate and imperial state, which ruled in the name of the "free market," understood as natural and thus beyond ideological critique or promotion.

Garrow's excellent research on Obama's community organizing and state legislative career in Illinois shows the future president claiming to address poverty and joblessness by increasing the market value of poor and jobless folks' "human capital" and "skill sets." Never does one learn of any serious call by Obama for the democratic redistribution of wealth and power or the advance of a people's political economy based on solidarity and the common good.

There are curious omissions in *Rising Star*, however. The otherwise meticulous Garrow never quotes either the widely read 2006 essay by Ken Silverstein ("Obama, Inc.") which was referenced in the present volume's third chapter or a remarkable essay by Larissa MacFarquhar published by *The New Yorker* in the spring of 2007. In early May of that year, six months after Obama had declared his candidacy for the White House, MacFarquhar penned a memorable portrait of Obama titled "The Conciliator: Where is Barack Obama Coming From?" "In his view of history, in his respect for tradition, in his skepticism that the world can be changed any way but very, very slowly," MacFarquhar wrote after extensive interviews with the candidate, "*Obama is deeply conservative.* There are moments when he sounds almost Burkean...It's not just that he thinks revolutions are unlikely: he *values continuity and stability for their own sake, sometimes even more than he values change for the good.*" [Emphasis added][2]

MacFarquhar's reflection is of particular relevance when it comes to understanding how pathetically passive Obama has been in response to the horrific far-right extremism of the Trump presidency. This is precisely the cringeworthy Obama now on display, who had this to say when the African-American finance capitalist Mellody Hobson asked him a reprise of Lenin's famous question "what is to be done?," at the Economic Club of Chicago eleven months into Trump's nightmare presidency:

> Hobson: Some of these institutions that we take for granted, …these institutions that the are the pillars of the American system…are being challenged very vocally, very loudly… even in our own country they are being second-guessed…

> Obama: yeah [stated reluctantly and skeptically]…

> Hobson: Do you think that those institutions have a real risk today of …[long pause] going away? Is there a real threat to [our] core values? And what do you do about that today? What concrete thing instead of, you know, we all are talking so much about what we are seeing, *What is to be done?*

> Obama: Well, look, look. It's important not to over-romanticize things, so what I talk about the values, ideals, institutions that I revere, the things that make me most proud to be an American, um, it's important to understand that those have always been contested and there's always been competing narratives in our country just like there is around the world. It wasn't that long ago that you and I would not be sitting here in front of the Economic Club [a reference to Obama and Hobson's shared technical Blackness]

> Hobson: But…[largely inaudible but clearly protesting]…

> Obama: Well, but, but the point is that the progress we make in strengthening these institutions is real but episodically at junctures in our history, whether because we're afraid or because of external threats or what have you, they start teetering a little bit. Look, FDR is one my political heroes. In my mind, he's the second greatest president, after Lincoln. But he interred a bunch of loyal Japanese-Americans during World War II. …There have been periods in our history when censorship was considered okay. We had the McCarthy era. We had a president who had to resign prior to impeachment because he was undermining rule of law. At every juncture, we've had to wrestle with big problems, dating back to the Constitution, the founding document, that was revolutionary but also contained the

> three-fifths clause. So we've always had some contradictions. That's part of human life. The question, then, is at any given time what are we doing to defend our best selves and those timeless values that should transcend party. So I would argue, for example, that freedom of the press is such an ideal....what I understood [as president] was that the principle of the free press was vital, and that as president part of my job was to make sure that that was maintained. And so, we don't have time to go into everything people should do, but I wouldn't underestimate the very simple act of being engaged, paying attention, and speaking out. Typically, that's what it comes down to in a democracy.[3]

This was an extraordinary statement of political and moral cowardice. Listening to this talk online, the present writer, an author (like Obama!) of two previous books on Obama, could not help feeling that little had changed in Obama's worldview. There was indeed, in MacFarquhar's words, a "deeply conservative" continuity between pre-presidential, presidential, and post-presidential Obama, despite Trump's unadulterated onslaught against the very institutions Obama claimed to cherish and revere.

Let's go back, then, to the moment at which Obama spoke to the Economic Club of Chicago. Obama's fascistic successor, the relentless Donald Trump, had already wreaked enormous havoc across the nation and world, and was poised to do yet more horrific and unspeakable damage to "democratic" and even merely republican institutions and values, not to mention assaulting basic moral precepts and common decency. After even a capitalist financier, clearly uneasy about the Trump administration and its odious intentions, asked him the Russian communist Vladimir Lenin's question, "What is to be done?," Obama could only say that history moves slowly and unevenly, with democratic "narratives" recurrently challenged by reactionary ones. "Sure," Obama was basically saying, "we've had slavery. We sent loyal citizens into concentration camps. McCarthyism unjustly ruined thousands of Americans' lives. But look, I was president even though I'm Black and my interviewer is up here at an elite venue even though she's Black. History moves forward. People need to pay attention and speak out and that will keep democracy alive even if things go backwards sometimes."

It was a horrific performance that received loud applause from the audience, comprised of Chicago's corporate and financial elite. Besides trivializing and normalizing white-nationalist and arch-authoritarian Trump's variation of fascism and pathetically failing to call out Trump by name, Obama's talk completely omitted his own lethal moves against press freedom and pretended that the corporate-plutocratic United States was home to a functioning democracy. It was, and is, home to no such thing, as a vast collection of carefully and heavily documented political and social science research shows.

But there was nothing remotely surprising here or in Obama's more general conduct during the Trump years. It was simply Obama being Obama. It was just the same old "deeply conservative" (Larissa MacFarquhar), "vacuous to repressive" (Adolph Reed, Jr.), and "brown-faced Clinton" (Cornel West) corporate Democrat that a host of progressive writers and activists had been warning Americans and the global community about since well before the Obama ascended to the presidency—since the summer of 2004, in my case. It was Obama showing his "dollar value" to the metropolitan business elite who did so much to launch the Obama phenomenon in the first place, and who now stood to profit handsomely from Trump's enormous regressive tax cut at the end of 2017.

Ex-president Obama's creation of rhetorical space for the white-nationalist Trump and his neo-fascism, both of which Obama did not deign to name, is part of the normal reactionary "counter-narrative" in a version of American history that is mainly about "progress" towards " a more perfect union"—all of it richly consistent with the "progressive" poseur about whom my fellow portsiders and I had warned even as he rose to national prominence during the second George W. Bush administration. One thing U.S. Senator and presidential candidate Obama had no shortage of was Orwellian chutzpah while he whitewashed American history on behalf of the nation's corporate and imperial masters. "If Americans have rejected" Thomas Jefferson's advice "to engage in a revolution every two or three generations," Obama wrote in his 2006 campaign book *The Audacity of Hope*, this was "only because the Constitution itself proved a sufficient defense against tyranny" (p. 93).

There was no room in that formulation for a large number of facts relevant to the distinctive weakness of radicalism in U.S. history, nor room for reflection on America's rich historical record of repressing radicals (e.g. Haymarket, the Palmer Raids, McCarthyism, COINTELPRO), nor consideration of the extreme racial, ethnic, religious, and territorial fragmentation of the nation's working class and general populace. The alternately deadening and co-optive influences of imperialism, mass consumerism, winner-take-all electoral politics, corporate media, and more found no place in Obama's story of America. Finally, there was no room for the remarkable persistence of business-class tyranny and white-supremacist rule, the reign of the military sector, or for the rise of a powerful prison-industrial system—all defining features of the U.S. today.

Obama's *Audacity* was impressively committed to misrepresenting the American past in accord with dominant national doctrine. He cited early Americans' purported faith in "self-reliance," "hard work," and "free will" (p. 54) as the source of the early Republic's "free market" development, ignoring slavery's role in (a) violating the nation's proclaimed republican virtues and (b) laying a critical foundation of capital for the early expansion of the American "free market" empire.

Furthermore, Obama wrote warmly of the "grand compromise" (p.75) found in the Constitutional bargain between the Northern and the Southern states—the one that approved and solidified black chattel slavery as the core, defining, and federally protected political-economic institution of the U.S. South.

He deftly inserted "property rights" (p. 86) into his list of the great "individual liberties" guaranteed by the Founders, deleting a critical conflict that shaped the early republic. That conflict, of course, was between human rights and property rights, the latter referring to the special, structurally super-empowered citizenship rights granted to the relatively small part of the population that owned large amounts of property.

Obama's *Audacity* audaciously and falsely conflated "democracy" with "the republican form of government" that the Founders preferred as an effective barrier to their ultimate nightmare: popular democracy, which they often equated to "mob rule." Obama appeared (pretended) not to know that the nation's constitutional founders saw republican governance as a bulwark against democracy and a more reliable protector of "property rights" and class privilege than monarchical absolutism. And he misrepresented the main reason that James Madison, Alexander Hamilton, and other Founders argued for a geographically extensive nation-state: to more effectively preserve the tyranny of the propertied few and keep the threat of popular democracy at bay (pp. 87–94).

The title of Obama's 2006 book was stolen from a sermon by his former "beloved pastor" Reverend Jeremiah Wright, whom candidate Obama would later throw under the bus after Wright's anti-imperialist sentiments were aired in the mainstream media. And Obama even misrepresented the views of the president he claimed to place first in the pantheon of great Americans, Abraham Lincoln. Lincoln, according Obama, was "unyielding in his opposition to slavery," which even a cursory reading of Lincoln's writings and speeches would have shown to be false. (p. 97)

The Audacity of Hope even praised the militant racist Woodrow Wilson for seeing that "it was in America's interest to encourage the self-determination of all peoples and provide the world a legal framework that could help avoid future conflicts" (p. 283). Too bad the Wilson administration's extreme racism found expression in the brutal U.S. invasions of Haiti and the Dominican Republic. As Noam Chomsky has noted, "Wilson's troops murdered, destroyed, reinstituted virtual slavery and demolished the constitutional system in Haiti." These actions followed in accord with the belief of Wilson's Secretary of State, Robert Lansing, that "the African race are devoid of any capacity for political organization" and possessed "an inherent tendency to revert to savagery and to cast aside the shackles of civilization which are irksome to their physical nature." Moreover, it was during Wilson's tenure that several agencies of the federal government were segregated in keeping with Wilson's views that Blacks constituted "an ignorant and inferior race."

Obama's *Audacity* honored U.S. Cold War foreign policymakers for combining "Wilsonian idealism" with "humility regarding America's ability to control events around the world" (p. 284). Without naming them, he justified such lovely examples of that "humility"—the U.S. overthrow of democratically elected governments in Iran (1953) and Guatemala (1954), for example, and the sponsorship of mass-murderous dictatorships in Indonesia and Latin American—by recycling the imperial myth that the U.S. was protecting the world against an expansionist and totalitarian Soviet Union (p. 284).

Obama's *Audacity* said that "the biggest casualty" of the Vietnam War was "the bond of trust between the American people and their government—and between American themselves," not, tellingly, the three to five million Vietnamese, Cambodians, and Laotians slaughtered by the U.S. crucifixion of Southeast Asia. Given his callous and willfully ignorant take on Vietnam, a "mistake" Obama blamed for helping generate the supposed "radical excesses" of 1960s protests, it was hardly surprising that Obama's *Audacity of Hope* was incapable of accurately identifying the George W. Bush administration's illegal, racist, and brazenly imperialist invasion of Iraq as a monumental war crime committed on brazenly false pretexts to deepen U.S. control of super-strategic Middle Eastern energy resources. In Obama's intentionally myopic view, Bush's invasion was a great strategic blunder—a "dumb" and "botched" (p.308) war, not a criminal one, and it was carried out with "the best of [democratic] intentions" (pp. 290–309). It was a mistaken effort "to impose democracy with the barrel of a gun" (p. 317).

The *Audacity of Hope* was neither Obama's first not his last exercise in power-and self-serving historical deletion and distortion. He kept it up all through his 2007–08 campaign, his election night victory speech, his presidency, his Farewell Address, and now his retirement.

Is this about personal weakness and cowardice, as Obama's leading biographer (Garrow) and former lover Sheila Jager believe? Perhaps, to some degree. The deeper reality is that Obama's "deeply conservative" beliefs have reflected either a calculated or perhaps a heartfelt allegiance to corporate "free market" ideals and the related "pragmatic" ruling/professional-class values inculcated and absorbed at Harvard Law, in the corporate-captive foundation world, and through his many contacts in the elite business sector and the foreign policy establishment as he rose through the American system. Along with a bottomless commitment to the American imperial project, those power-serving beliefs were pervasive and thematic and not just in *The Audacity of Hope* (whose right-wing and imperial content Garrow ignores). They also served as the connecting threads in his famous 2004 Democratic Convention Keynote Address that did so much to make Obama an overnight national and even global celebrity. This was another document whose right-leaning ideological nature[4] escapes Garrow's attention.

Just as Obama's corporate and imperial ideology are missing from *Rising Star*, so too are the many left activists and writers, this writer included, who saw through Obama's progressive pretense and warned others about it early on.[5] Also largely missing in Garrow's account is the elite corporate and financial class, which understood that Obama was on their side and made record-setting contributions to his political rise. How does an author write a 1000-page plus account of Obama's rise to power without at least mentioning the august and unparalleled ruling class figure Robert Rubin, whose nod of approval was critical to Obama's ascendancy? As Greg Palast noted, the former Goldman Sachs CEO and Council on Foreign Relations head Rubin "opened the doors to finance industry vaults for Obama. Extraordinarily for a Democrat, Obama in 2008 raised three times as much from bankers as his Republican opponent." Rubin would also serve as a top informal Obama adviser, and he successfully placed a number of his own protégés in high-ranking positions in the Obama administration. Among Rubin's appointees to Obama's staff included Timothy Geithner (Obama's first Treasury Secretary), Peter Orszag (Obama's first Office of Management and Budget director), and Larry Summers (first chief economic adviser).

Do the "deeply conservative" limits of Obama's Weimar-like presidency and his cringingly Trump-normalizing post-presidency stem from a "need to be loved and admired" (Sheila Jager)? There are reasons to question that psycho-historical narrative. Surely the need would have been met to no small degree had Obama acted on his declared admiration for the New Deal president Franklin Delano Roosevelt (Obama's "second greatest president" after Abraham Lincoln) by governing in at least partial accord with the progressive-sounding rhetoric he campaigned on in 2007 and 2008. Beyond the social, democratic, and environmental benefits that millions of Americans and world citizens would have experienced under an actually progressive Obama presidency, such policy would have been good politics for both Obama and the Democratic Party. It might also have pre-empted the Tea Party rebellion and helped to keep the beastly Donald Trump out of the White House. The bigger problem here was Obama's love and admiration for the nation's reigning elite, or, perhaps, his reasonable calculation that the powers that be held a monopoly on the means for bestowing public love and admiration. Non-conformism to ruling class interests carries no small cost in a political culture owned by the incorporated possessing classes. Ask Bernie Sanders and Ralph Nader.

The ruling class has no interest in promoting the legacy of an ex-president who tells the truth about how the American system put him at the pinnacle of political power, and how it subsequently installed and maintained a neo-fascist in the same position. The ruling class prefers ex-presidents (and presidents) who don't rock the boat, and who play by the rules of corporate-managed pseudo-democracy and its narrow, savagely time-staggered major-party election "choices." Obama is more than willing to comply with the role to which he is assigned as ex-president. He has become accustomed to the task after many years of behaving in accord with the nation's corporate and financial masters, both before and during his presidency. That is simply Obama being Obama, a "hollow" man filled with ruling class ideas.

ENDNOTES

1. David Garrow, *Bearing the Cross: Martin Luther King Jr. and the Southern Leadership Conference*: William Morrow, 1986

2. MacFarquhar cited as an example of this reactionary sentiment Obama's reluctance to embrace single-payer health insurance on the Canadian model, which he told her would "so disruptive that people feel like suddenly what they've known for most of their lives is thrown by the wayside." Obama told MacFarquhar that "we've got all these legacy systems in place, and managing the transition, as well as adjusting the culture to a different system, would be difficult to pull off. So we may need a system that's not so disruptive that people feel like suddenly what they've known for most of their lives is thrown by the wayside." So what if large popular majorities in the U.S. had long favored the single-payer model? So what if single payer would let people keep the doctors of their choice, only throwing away the protection pay off to the

private insurance mafia? So what if "the legacy systems" Obama defended included corporate insurance and pharmaceutical oligopolies that regularly threw millions of American lives by the wayside of market calculation, causing enormous disruptive harm and death for the populace?

3. "Barack Obama at the Economic Club of Chicago," YouTube, uploaded December 8, 2017. https://www.youtube.com/watch?v=McfvFMXN7Is

4. For real-time left content analysis and critique, see Paul Street, "Keynote Reflections," *ZNet*, July 29, 2004, https://zcomm.org/znetarticle/keynote-reflections-by-paul-street/

5. The list of Left commentators left out is long. It includes Bruce Dixon, Glen Ford, John Pilger, Noam Chomsky, Ken Silverstein, Alexander Cockburn, Margaret Kimberly, Jeffrey St. Clair, Roger Hodge, Pam Martens, Ajamu Baraka, Doug Henwood, Juan Santos, Marc Lamont Hill, John R. MacArthur, and a host of others. See the sub-section titled "Insistent Left Warnings" on pages 176–177 in the sixth chapter, titled "We Were Warned," of my 2010 book *The Empire's New Clothes: Barack Obama in the Real World of Power* (New York: Routledge, 2010), a second heavily researched Obama book not to make it into Garrow's endnotes or bibliography.

CONCLUSION

The "apocalypse" that Barack Obama told his staffers (as well as David Remnick) *wasn't* coming with the ascendancy of Donald Trump has certainly come to America in 2020, if it didn't already arrive at the beginning of Trump's reign. Trump is a fascist death machine. He's proved it again and again in numerous ways—ways that have been recounted at length in this volume.

Given the endlessly reckless, disease-, death-, and Depression-driving lunacy of the wannabe fascist dictator who sits in the world's most powerful office, it is unsurprising that his approval rating is in the tank—a remarkably low 37–39% four months out from a presidential election. Two-thirds of the nation, a super-majority, disapproves of how Trump has handled the COVID-19 pandemic.

Also unsurprisingly, Democratic presidential nominee Joe Biden leads Trump in key battleground states (the only places where a real presidential election happens, thanks to the absurdly undemocratic Electoral College system). Biden is running even with Trump even in some traditionally "red" (Republican) states, like COVID-19-riddled Texas, as this book goes to press.

Real unemployment may be as high as 20% as the economy sinks into another Great Depression sparked by a deadly public health crisis that Trump and his Republican allies have viciously fueled and then lied about. Nearly three-quarters (72%) of Americans say the U.S. is "on the wrong track."

The numbers don't look good for the man who Obama privately called a "fascist" during the 2016 campaign, only to subsequently tell Americans to welcome the beast as their next president (since "we're all Americans first") the day after Trump won.

So, "Trump is toast," as numerous liberals and some lefties have been telling this author for the last year or so. Are they right? Maybe. But not necessarily. Hillary Clinton looked like a "sure thing" to defeat Trump in the summer of 2016. I'm not making any predictions this time around. Maddening as the prospect of a second Trump term may be, it remains a distinct possibility for at least four reasons.

First, there's the sheer corporatist, imperialist, and clumsily racist awfulness of Joe Biden, detailed at length in this book's fifth chapter. Biden's egregious record as a cringing corporate pet, a white-supremacist, and a vicious hawk will make it difficult for many progressives to vote for him for any reason other than the simple fact that he isn't Donald Trump. Shame on Barack Obama and the rest of the Democratic establishment for putting this 77-year old, right-wing, out-of-step candidate up as the answer to Trump's authoritarian reign. In addition to his abysmal record of serving the interests of corporate campaign contributors and the military-industrial complex, Biden has also shown indications of incipient dementia, spewing forth enough incoherencies, mala-propisms, and inappropriate comments to keep YouTube viewers howling in laughter or cringing in embarrassment. (And I should note, this is not me hypothesizing on Biden's mental condition. This is the position of numerous professionals I have consult-ed). This is the Democratic establishment's answer to a president that Noam Chomsky rightly calls "the most dangerous criminal in human history"? It's not for nothing that the Democrats are keeping Biden as far out of the public eye as humanly possible this summer and fall. They have no idea what kind of verbal screw-ups he may put out on the airwaves and Internet, and what kind of fodder he may provide the Trump campaign as it seeks to highlight Biden's apparent mental deficiencies.

Second, there's the astonishing amount of money ($416 million just by the end of June of 2020 and certain to top $ 1 billion before the election) that is being pumped into the Trump noise and hate machine by billionaires and multi-millionaires pleased with his regressive tax cuts, his ongoing efforts "dismantle the regulatory state," and his sweetheart deals for corporate friends. Trump's giant billionaire-funded war chest will pay for a head-spinning and truth-trashing blitzkrieg of neo-McCarthyite and nativist attack ads and "social media" gaslighting. Look for Trump's deep-pockets campaign to connect Biden to "the Chinese Communist Party," "Antifa," the "radical Left," and "the Chinese virus." It certainly would not be out of the realm of possibility for Trump's media-savvy cohort of campaign prevaricators to claim that Biden and the "radical Democrats" have been conspiring with China to defeat Trump by creating an unprecedented virus that has sickened and killed tens of thousands of Americans and decimated the "greatest economy in history." Repeated often enough, such paranoid and seemingly absurd messaging could take hold with a portion of the electorate, especially in an environment where lying and deception have become standard political practice. Trump and his campaign will of course also relentlessly attack Biden's mental fitness, an ironic strategy given Trump's own malignant narcissism and obvious intellectual deficiencies.

Republican campaign messaging will of course relentlessly absolve Trump of any responsibility for the economic pain being felt by tens of millions of Americans, a position Trump himself has already staked out by laying blame on China and Democrat naysayers. The Trump Depression and the resulting mass suffering will be treated as nothing more than the accidental (and unfortunate) outcome of a virus imposed on "great" America by evil China, linked in campaign rhetoric to Biden, Obama, and the "radical Left" Democratic Party.

Third, there's the near certainty that Trump and co-conspirators like Attorney General William Barr will concoct some sort of big "October Surprise" akin to the James Comey/FBI revelations that helped sink Hillary Clinton in 2016. Expect high-profile

"Obamagate" prosecutions of former Obama administration officials in Barr's forthcoming *Durham Report*, likely to be released before the election. Also, don't be surprised if the Trump administration cynically claims at the last moment that "Operation Warp Speed" is a miraculous success and a pandemic-weary electorate is presented with an unverified COVID-19 vaccine or cure, whose efficacy won't be known until after the ballots have been counted.

Fourth, given his low standing in national and battleground state polls vis-à-vis even Joe Biden, the widely hated Trump and his henchmen will do everything in their considerable powers they can to obstruct and discourage a fair and democratic election this fall. There is a slight but more than negligible possibility that Trump will use the very pandemic that he has dismissed and yet done so very much to exacerbate, or some other "national emergency" either real or fake, in a bid to suspend the November elections. He could declare the coronavirus a crisis requiring the suspension of the elections for public health reasons—no small irony. He will repeatedly reiterate his false claim that mail-in-ballots—the obvious fix for virus-necessitated prohibitions on in-person voting—are inherently subject to fraud. In an insantly infamous Tweet at the end of July 2020, Trump floated the idea of suspending the election because of mail-in voting's supposedly flawed nature.

Most ominously of all, perhaps, it was clear by the time this volume went to press that Trump was trying to manufacture self-fulfilling evidence for his thesis by having his recently appointed Postmaster General Louis DeJoy (a major Trump donor and fundraiser) produce mail backlogs meant to demonstrate that the U.S. Postal Service is "a mess" (Trump's description) and therefore incapable of processing ballots in a fair and timely fashion. It's an authoritarian two-fer. The point is to discourage voting ("it's going to be a big uncountable fiasco so why bother?") and to discredit a potential Biden victory in preparation of a legal challenge advanced by Trump's fascist Attorney General William Barr. If he can't cancel or suspend the election, Trump wants a long period of uncertainty after a vote not to his liking, a period in which he, his minions, and his white-nationalist (Republican) party can manipulate events.

Sickeningly enough, COVID-19 may be part of the strategy. If anything, the virulent racist and Social Darwinist president has been encouraged to let the virus spread by data showing (as explained to him by white supremacists like his top political adviser Stephen Miller) that COVID-19 most particularly kills the poor, vulnerable, and nonwhite. But there are related electoral/anti-electoral considerations as well. We know from a recent in-depth *Vanity Fair* report that Trump's sociopathic son-and-law Jared Kushner squashed a plan for national coronavirus testing last March and April after determining that the virus was hitting Democratic states the hardest and that the White House would be able to blame its spread on the nation's fifty state governors.

It's not for nothing that Trump's party has been trying to assemble an army of 50,000 "poll watchers" for November, "part of a multimillion-dollar effort to police who votes and how" (NBC News). The "poll watchers" will be brutish voter-intimidators specially deployed to minority polling locations in key battleground cities.

Also menacing in its implications for a fair election are Trump's decision in late July to send fascistic federal paramility forces to a number of Democratic cities under the name "Operation Legend." Four of the six cities to which these federal agents have been sent under the dubious pretext of combatting Black-on-Black violence are located in electorally contested battleground states: Milwaukee, Albequerque, Detroit, and Cleveland.

These are the kinds of frankly nefarious things a fascist U.S. president would be expected to do when facing an election he thinks he can't win in "normal" ways. Liberal media commentators' and Democratic politicos' insistent claims at the end of July that Trump "can't" suspend the election "because of the Constitution" seem possibly naive in light of the Trump administration and Attorney General Barr's long and clearly demonstrated contempt for constitutional checks and balances, not to mention for the rule of law. It is true that the U.S. Constitution does not permit Trump to suspend or cancel a nationl election. But if top military commanders were convinced that just cause exists for suspending or cancelling the election, then Trump could do it. Even without an actual suspension, the declaration of a national emergency could create an environment in which vast swaths of the electorate were kept away from voting places. As this manuscript neared completion in late July, Trump deployed federal paramilitaries in what one big city mayor called "a dress rehearsal for martial law," as we have seen.

If the election is held, as it mostly likely will be, there will still be big problems with taking and counting the ballots. There will be the standard racist and partisan voter suppression, silence over which remains a longstanding gentleman's agreement between the major parties. Republicans have shown their determination to suppress the nonwhite and Democratic vote in Wisconsin and Georgia this year. The majority-Republican U.S. Supreme Court ruled this July that Florida can block hundreds of thousands of predominantly Black felons from voting, making it unlikely that they will be allowed to cast their ballots in the presidential election. We must expect much the same thing and worse in November. Practical voter-access and ballot-counting difficulties related to the complexities of holding a national election amidst a pandemic will only add to the difficulties in trying to get a true count.

Trump will challenge the legitimacy of an Electoral College count that does not go his way. Trump has been seeding the narrative that he cannot be fairly voted out of office from day one of his twisted reign. With the arch-authoritarian, white-nationalist,

Barr taking the lead, the Trump administration will almost certainly challenge a Biden victory in the courts. And if there's one thing Trump has shown, it is that he's extremely skilled at using the court system to frustrate his opponents. Millions could hit the streets outraged, leading Trump to invoke the 1807 Insurrection Act and deploy federal troops against "radical Left terrorists." The ball could pass into the hands of the nation's top military commanders, with an uncertain outcome, especially if Biden's victory margin is small. Local, county, and state police forces, instinctually and institutionally fascist, can be expected to side with the monster Trump. And in testimony given to Congress in late July of this year, Barr would not commit his office to honoring the outcome of an election Trump failed to win.

But even if Trump is successfully voted out and can be compelled to leave without incident—as is certainly possible (especially if Biden's scores a landslide popular vote and Electoral College victory)—the wisdom of Howard Zinn will remain essential. "The really critical thing," Zinn once said, "isn't who is sitting in the White House, but who is sitting in—in the streets, in the cafeterias, in the halls of government, in the factories. Who is protesting, who is occupying offices and demonstrating—those are the things that determine what happens."

This wise counsel still applies if the corporate clown Joe Biden becomes the nation's forty-sixth president on January 20, 2021. Nothing remotely progressive will happen under a Biden-Harris administration without masses of people regularly demanding change in the streets, on the shop floors, in the town centers, and in the halls of government. Another miserable center-right corporate presidency on the model of Bill Clinton and Barack Obama will be met by a neofascistic reaction and could very possibly translate into a successor presidency (Tom Cotton?) so vicious and right-wing as to make some people nostalgic for the Trump years, absurd as that sounds.

It is perfectly understandable and very much to be expected that millions of progressive and liberal voters will hold their noses to vote "for" Biden to block the fascist Trump. Who left of the Trumpenvolk wants a second term for the indecent orange beast? At the same time, the routine quadrennial argument of Left intellectuals that responsible citizens must vote for Democrats as the "lesser evil" often becomes a viciously circular and self-fulfilling prophecy that helps advance the very thing its fears: hard-right corporate authoritarianism and even, as we witness now, unvarnished neofascism. Left "Lesser Evil Voting" (LEV) is plagued by two critical flaws. First, the standard progressive practice of sheepishly promising one's vote without conditions to corporate and imperialist Democrats ("lying neoliberal warmongers," to use Adolph Reed, Jr's apt description of Hilly Clinton in the late summer of 2016) helps push the Democratic Party further to the starboard side, thereby rendering it ever-more out of touch with the nation's progressive majority. Moreover, by allowing a rightward shift in Democratic politics, the "lesser evil" option opens the door to Republicans by demobilizing otherwise left-leaning Democratic voters. As Glenn Greenwald, the brilliant critic of Obama and the Democratic Party, has argued, citizens lose their leverage when they grant unconditional support to politicians: "They have no reason to do anything but ignore you with contempt because you've put yourself in a subservient position... When you say, 'I don't care how much you trample on my values, I'm still going to vote for you.' Why would anybody listen to a group of people who say that?" Politicians have no reason to make concessions to people who have in essence already pledged to vote for them anyway. The entire process becomes a vicious circle. "If you continue to empower and support and fortify this neoliberal, corporatist, militarist wing of a party over and over and over again...Gore...Kerry...Obama...Hillary Clinton... Now we're supporting Joe Biden," Greenwald asks, "what is the point of politics if that's what you're doing?"

Second, LEV also helps ratchet the Republican Party ever further to the apocalyptic and neo-fascistic right as the Democrats steal more and more of the Republicans' onetime pro-business, imperial, and authoritarian agenda. Even as they reasonably denounce the scary dreadfulness of the right-most party, left "Lesser-Evilists" are encouraging the drift of Republicans into fascist, white-nationalist territory. It's the only space the Republicans have left in a party system that has gone far to the right of the citizenry. The two-party system has veered so far to the right partly because of LEV.

Even when the Inauthentic Opposition (Democratic Party) manages to take power, as it did in 2009 and certainly could do in 2021, its abject servility to Wall Street, corporate America, and the military-industrial-police state complex can be counted on to seed the terrain for future white-nationalist triumphs. As *Counterpunch* writer Bruce Levine wrote last June:

> Noam Chomsky is quite right to warn us of a fascist apocalypse, but it may be worse than Trump. The 2016 Trump election resulted, in large part, from a corporatist Democratic Party's abandonment of the 99%. The corporatist-friendly Bill Clinton created the conditions for Bush-Cheney, and a corporatist-friendly Barack Obama and Hillary Clinton created the conditions for Trump. What kind of hell-on-earth nightmare do we get with the conditions created by a corporatist-bootlicking Biden administration?

It's an excellent question. Americans may find themselves practically missing the Trump years (!) if and when the dismal, dollar-drenched corporate Democratic Biden administration gives way to the white-nationalist presidency of someone the likes of Tom Cotton, a U.S. Senator and Harvard Law graduate who is every bit as far right as Donald Trump but has the ability to wrap his fascistic world view in elegant-sounding and silver-tongued prose.

So, vote third party? The present author has done that in ten of the last eleven presidential elections and may well do so (in a "safely" Democratic state) again this year (if a vote is held). But there's not much point in pretending that third party candidates enjoy any chance of success under the American winner-take-all two-party system. People who want viable third party candidacies need to get serious about a constitutional overhaul—including the mandatory full public financing of elections and the implementation of proportional representation, among other changes—that allows space for third and fourth parties to become sustainably potent players in voicing popular sentiments and making policy. Without constitutional transformation, third party campaigns are doomed. For what it's worth, most Americans polled have long correctly believed that the two dominant political parties do not reflect the actual spectrum of poliltical opinion in the U.S. As very few Americans know, a number of brilliant constitutional lawyers, legal theorists, and activists have long been doing impressive work on what constitutional change of the kind that would allow viable third and fourth parties would look like, and how to make it happen.

I understand very well why many on the portside will vote for Biden in order to block Trump, especially in the handful of states that remain truly contested. If I wasn't registered in a "safe state" (an amusing term in these wildly precarious times), I would consider it myself. This book argues, after all, that Trump is a fascist. It does not argue the same thing about Biden, despite his history of obsequious obedience to the interests of the rich and powerful. But, for me, as for many others on the American Left, electoral politics are simply not a major focus, given the frankly un- and even anti-democratic nature of the American political, economic, and social system, a reality that defines not only the current deadly moment but the entire expanse of US history. The nation is in dire need of a mass people's movement that focuses on the essential character of American society and goes beyond the quadrennial electoral spectacles that are sold to Americans as "that's politics"—the only politics that matters. As Chomsky wrote sixteen years ago on the eve of the only presidential election in which I consented (in a contested state) to do LEV:

> Americans may be encouraged to vote, but not to partici-
> pate more meaningfully in the political arena. Essentially
> the election is a method of marginalizing the population.
> A huge propaganda campaign is mounted to get people
> to focus on these personalized quadrennial extravaganzas
> and to think, "That's politics." But it isn't. It's only a small
> part of politics…The urgency is for popular progressive
> groups to grow and become strong enough so that centers
> of power can't ignore them. Forces for change that have
> come up from the grass roots and shaken the society to its
> core include the labor movement, the civil rights movement,
> the peace movement, the women's movement and others,
> cultivated by steady, dedicated work at all levels, every day,
> not just once every four years…[Election choices] are sec-
> ondary to serious political action. The main task is to create
> a genuinely responsive democratic culture, and that effort
> goes on before and after electoral extravaganzas, whatever
> their outcome.

As Zinn elaborated in a purple passage published in March 2008, just as "Obamamania" was peaking in the Democratic Party's primary electorate:

> Would I support one candidate against another? Yes, for
> two minutes—the amount of time it takes to pull the lever
> down in the voting booth. But before and after those two
> minutes, our time, our energy, should be spent in educating,
> agitating, organizing our fellow citizens in the workplace, in
> the neighborhood, in the schools…
>
> The Democrats offer no radical change from the status quo.
> They do not propose what the present desperation of people
> cries out for: a government guarantee of jobs to everyone
> who needs one, a minimum income for every household,
> housing relief to everyone who faces eviction or foreclosure.
> They do not suggest the deep cuts in the military budget

or the radical changes in the tax system that would free billions, even trillions, for social programs to transform the way we live.

...For instance, the mortgage foreclosures that are driving millions from their homes—they should remind us of a similar situation after the Revolutionary War, when small farmers, many of them war veterans (like so many of our homeless today), could not afford to pay their taxes and were threatened with the loss of the land, their homes. They gathered by the thousands around courthouses and refused to allow the auctions to take place.

The evictions today of people who cannot pay their rents should remind us of what people did in the Thirties when they organized and put the belongings of the evicted families back in their apartments, in defiance of the authorities.

Historically, government, whether in the hands of Republicans or Democrats, conservatives or liberals, has failed its responsibilities, until forced to by direct action: sit-ins and Freedom Rides for the rights of black people, strikes and boycotts for the rights of workers, mutinies and desertions of soldiers in order to stop a war.

Voting is easy and marginally useful, but it is a poor substitute for democracy, which requires direct action by concerned citizens.

For the present writer at least, the main problem with the Bernie Sanders candidacy wasn't merely that it was ultimately "sheep-dogging" progressive and left voters into the corporate Democratic Party. It was that the Sanders crusade was Judas-Goating progressive political energies into a narrow form of political engagement geared around two minutes in a voting booth once every 1,460 days. For all his references to a mass movement of supporters, Sanders nonetheless offered a model that began in the conventional electoral process and did little to transcend it. It is of course perfectly understandable that millions of Americans whose values and policy preferences stand well to the left of Biden will nonetheless vote to block the instinctual fascist, abject racist, miserable sexist, vicious nativist, and eco-exterminist Trump this November. But the key questions are what millions of Americans will do before and after those two minutes spent in the voting booth, and whether a critical mass of persistently militant Americans can broaden their sense of the change required to transform their society into something that can reasonably be described as just, sustainable, and democratic.

There's another and related matter that deserves mention: the fierce urgency of getting Trump out of the White House *now*. Assuming that it can happen, January 20, 2021 may well be too late to remove the reckless Trump malignancy from power. As this manuscript neared its conclusion in late July 2020, with its frankly Trump-exhausted author dreading the daily news of Trump's latest fascist offense and scanning for Obama's latest response or non-response, it was clear that the nation had landed in a very dangerous moment. With an election nearing and his approval numbers falling, thanks in large measure to his openly socio-pathological and vicious responses to the pandemic and the George Floyd people's rebellion, Trump had become a hazardously wounded animal. According to psychologist Craig Malkin, a contributor to a psychological study of Trump published after the last election, "The greatest danger [of Trump and people like him]...is that pathological narcissists can lose touch with reality in ways that become extremely dangerous over time. When they can't let go of their need to be admired or recognized, they have to bend or invent a reality in which they can remain special, despite all messages to the contrary. In point of fact, they become dangerously psychotic."

By the late summer and early fall of 2020, we are well past that psychotic tipping point with the fascist Donald Trump. As Seattle's mayor Jenny Durkan said in late July, as the White House declared its intent to send paramilitaries to confront protesters in her city, "it looks like this president is doing a dress rehearsal for martial law."

It is reckless and immoral to leave Trump in the White House until January 20, 2021. His administration is a clear and present danger to everyone and everything we hold dear on numerous levels. The "Trump Virus"—Nancy Pelosi's apt moniker for COVID-19 this summer—has already killed 170,000 Americans and may well kill half a million by January 20th of next year, In the face of the national Trump emergency we must act on a mass and sustained scale, demanding the end of the Trump-Pence regime now. We cannot wait, and the world cannot wait, more than one hundred days for this indecent beast and his fascist flying monkey of a vice president to be removed from power, assuming they'd agree to leave after losing a mere election. Think about how much more damage these lunatics can and will do if given 120 days.

As the sharp Left commentator and activist Arun Gupta wrote from the frontlines of the popular struggle against Trumpism-fascism in late July:

> Thousands of Americans in one city are openly rebelling against the government. And it's parents and nurses and Teamsters and line cooks and teachers and students. They are being joined by people streaming into Portland from all over the Western U.S. They get it. Trump's fascism needs to be crushed by the people. And it needs to be crushed now. I have been out half a dozen times in the last two weeks. The resistance is overwhelmingly nonviolent. They are facing down armed maniacs with homemade armor. They are extraordinarily courageous...I've been warning for three years that Trump is going to bring the war on terror home. It's begun in Portland. Yeah, these [people] want Trump out, even if that means being replaced by a neoliberal corpse named Joe Biden. *But if you think this can wait until November, that's like waiting for rescue ships to come to the aid of the Titanic.* Trump needs to be smashed to bits now with massive fierce nonviolent resistance like is happening in Portland right now every night. I'm old, out of shape and with a nagging injury that makes it hard to run. But I have to be out there because the determination of these kids is

extraordinary. They are fighting for you. They are fighting
for your kids and family. For every notion of freedom
and liberty you hold dear. Right here, right now. And you
need to be out there fighting as well. It will be too late in
November if we don't act now.

The esteemed Yale historian Timothy Snyder appeared to agree.
Snyder said this last July 24th when MSNBC's Rachel Maddow
asked him what was to be done about the nation's potential slide
into "authoritarianism":

...Protest...You have to start identifying yourself with the
protesters. So if first they come for the undocumented and
you do nothing because you're documented, you're making
a mistake. Then they come for the Blacks and you don't
do anything because you're not Black, you're making a
mistake. Then they come for the protesters and you don't do
anything, you're making a mistake. At some point you have
to turn it around and say, like those moms in Portland are
doing, if they're coming for the protesters I have to stand up
for my fellow people, my fellow Americans, their right to
the First Amendment, to the Fourth Amendment... History
shows that mass peaceful protest works. So if you're not
protesting now, this would be a good time to start.

People who say they participate in politics because they go
into a voting booth or use a mail-in ballot to make a mark next
to the name of a corporate and imperial Democrat once every
4 years are like somebody who says they've got a healthy diet
because they eat a single bowl of pesticide-laden spinach once
every 1,460 days.

Establishment elites like the nation's most popular living
Democrat, Barack Obama, have a simple fix for the flaws they
admit to: vote for Democrats on constitutionally appointed
election dates. Recall Obama's statement to University of Illinois
students in September of 2018: "The best way to protest is to
vote. When you vote," Obama said, "you've got the power." And
remember Obama's statement at John Lewis's funeral last July:

voting is "the most important action we can take on behalf of democracy."

Really? We get to vote, yes, but mammon reigns nonetheless in the United States, where, as the mainstream political scientists Benjamin Page and Martin Gilens note in their important book *Democracy in America?*, "government policy ... reflects the wishes of those with money, not the wishes of the millions of ordinary citizens who turn out every two years to choose among the preapproved, money-vetted candidates for federal office"— candidates like Obama, who blew up the public presidential campaign finance system with record-setting contributions from the likes of Goldman Sachs and Citigroup in 2008.

There has long been a self-destructive and frankly pathetic degree of intra-leftist bloodletting on how portsiders can best respond to the absurdly narrow range of choices on offer in the U.S. party and elections system. This venom among progressives and radicals is badly misplaced. The real and serious political question is about what we do before and after, not during elections. And this fall, it seems distinctly possible that mass action in the streets will be required even to secure an election outcome supposedly guaranteed by the U.S. Constitution. Trump has made it clear that he wants to be president for life and that he does not believe that he can be fairly voted out of office. To reiterate, Trump was clearly moving by the end of July to discredit and undermine the 2020 election, claiming falsely that the mail-in ballots required by the very pandemic he helped fan across the nation are inherently inaccurate and counterfeit—this while his right-wing Postmaster General created national mail delivery backlogs and his mercenary paramilitaries ran "dress rehearsals for martial law" in U.S. cities. It may well take organized and large-scale pressure with millions in streets to force him out of the White House. Don't look for Barack Obama to support the popular movement that may be required to remove the man he knew to be a fascist, who he helped install in the world's most powerful job.

Americans will need, however, to undertake a giant popular uprising that targets not just the Trump-Pence regime but the whole U.S. state-capitalist order and its vast imperial and repressive edifice at home and abroad—the broad institutional and cultural structures of oppression (including the Democratic Party) that *made something as noxious as a Donald Trump presidency possible in the first place.* As Chris Hedges wrote on the left Website *Truthdig* May of 2018:

> The Trump administration did not rise, *prima facie*, like Venus on a half shell from the sea. Donald Trump is the result of a long process of political, cultural and social decay. He is a product of our failed democracy. The longer we perpetuate the fiction that we live in a functioning democracy, that Trump and the political mutations around him are somehow an aberrant deviation that can be vanquished in the next election, the more we will hurtle toward tyranny. The problem is not Trump. It is a political system, dominated by corporate power and the mandarins of the two major political parties, in which we don't count. We will wrest back political control by dismantling the corporate state, and this means massive and sustained civil disobedience.... If we do not stand up, we will enter a new dark age.

The "real issue to be faced," Dr. Martin Luther King Jr. wrote in his final essay, "is the radical reconstruction of society itself." For King, whose bust sat disapprovingly behind Obama during the forty-fourth president's eight years in the White House, the price of not undertaking that task was a fascistic corporate war and police state. As King ruminated just months before his violent death:

> They'll throw us into concentration camps. The Wallaces and the Birchites will take over. The sick people and the fascists will be strengthened. They'll cordon off the ghetto and issue passes for us to get in and out....We cannot stand two

more summers like last summer without leading inevitably to a rightwing takeover and a fascist state that will destroy the soul of the nation. To prevent this, we're going to be militant.

The "new dark age" may well already be underway. It is long past time for a real American Revolution. What have we got to lose?